Seeking Soul Mates, Spirit Guides, and Past Lives

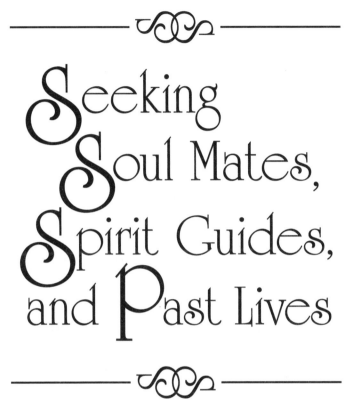

Previous Works

Books

Turning Trauma Into Triumph:
Ten Stories of Hope and Growth, Including My Own

Other Titles by Richard C. Scheinberg

Four Simple Ways To Overcome Depression DVD

Seeking Soul Mates, Spirit Guides, and Past Lives

Richard C. Scheinberg, LCSW, BCD

Legwork Team Publishing
New York

Legwork Team Publishing
80 Davids Drive, Suite 1
Hauppauge, NY 11788
www.legworkteam.com
Phone: 631- 944-6511

**Legwork Team
Publishing**

First edition 4/20/2009

ISBN: 978-0-5780-1866-9 (sc)
ISBN: 978-0-5780-1865-2 (hc)

Printed in the United States of America

This book is printed on acid-free paper.

This book is dedicated to my father, Irving
Scheinberg, my sister Lynne Harrell,
my brother, Gerry Harrell, and my
great-grandmother Berta Henry,
all of whom have communicated their love
and wisdom to me from the other side.

I would also like to offer a special dedication to
my mother, Mary Kathryn Scheinberg, who
crossed over just a few months ago. She always
gave me confidence and told me I could grow up
to do anything if I tried. So to my mom I want to
say, "I thank you for your eternal love
and inspiration."

Acknowledgments

Over the years there have been hundreds of people who have touched my heart and prompted me to do some soul-searching in one way or another. My openness and my career choice have fostered this awareness. I have now come to understand that even when I was young, naïve and in pain, they were there with me all along, just waiting to be discovered.

Among those I would like to thank most are my wife Geraldine, my son Jared, and the members of both my extended family and my adopted family of close friends. You have shown me so much love and kindness over the years, even when I may have not recognized it as such. Your overwhelming love and support cannot be adequately described or quantified. I would like to offer special thanks to Laura Berhalter, who met with me every Sunday evening for this labor of love—the completion of this manuscript. Her dedication and insightful feedback were always much appreciated. Sharon Sivak also contributed countless hours offering editing suggestions for this work. Her artful contributions and poetic talents cannot be overstated. Finally, many thanks are due to Yvonne Kamerling and Janet Yudewitz of the Legwork Team, who were instrumental in preparing the final draft of this book for publication.

I must also acknowledge my gratitude to God, my angels, and spirit guides who have given me guidance from the other side. Your presence has become evident to me from time to time while awake or asleep, sometimes vividly or subtly, but always when asked or when I needed you most.

Lastly, I would like to thank those spiritual teachers who have given me cause to pause and reflect during the most challenging times of my life. Among the hundreds who have brought passionate messages to the written page, I have been fortunate to personally attend workshops and retreats with many current luminaries including Carolyn Myss, Dr. Raymond Moody, James Van Praagh, Deepak Chopra, Doreen Virtue, Dr. Norman Shealy, Steven Farmer, Hank Wesselman, Sean David Morton, and many others. As you'll see in this book, Char Margolis and Dr. Brian Weiss, along with his wife Carol, have also had a dramatic impact on my life's spiritual path.

My heartfelt thanks go out to all of you. Whether you realize it or not, you each have been an integral part of my personal growth and sustenance. All of you have kept the fire lit within me during my discovery of all the eternal, loving relationships in this miraculous journey called life.

A Note to the Reader

Psychotherapist-client confidentiality is a strong and time-honored principle of practice ethics. Therefore, the names and certain identifying details of the clients mentioned in this book have been altered in order to protect their privacy.

Contents

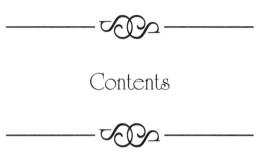

Prologue

What is going on in the world? We live crowded, busy lives that often leave us feeling empty and alone. Material wealth and creature comforts fail to truly satisfy our needs or make us happy. We eat, drink, and indulge our five senses to excess and yet life's "fullness" eludes us. This is as true within our individual families as it is in the global community. Have we just lost sight of what is really important?

I have come to believe that the real solutions to our problems must also include that which we cannot verify using only our five senses. There is a whole world that is invisible to us but essential to our survival, just like the air we breathe.

Our Life Force is composed of core energy. This energy, like all energy, can never be destroyed. The vessel of this energy is the soul, in concert with the Divine Force of the Universe. The soul does not die when the physical body ceases to function; the soul's identity and energy continues to exist in a new form. And in this new form, the soul can and often does continue to interact with those of us who remain here in the physical world.

This book is intended for those who have heard the words "soul mates," "spirit guides," and "past lives" and wondered if they are just new age buzzwords or if life beyond the flesh really exists. I invite you to explore and consider the possibilities that these concepts suggest. Read about the hidden relationships that may be affecting your life and may explain your personality, life path, and even your life's purpose. Let my words arouse your curiosity and provoke you to do some deep soul-searching. Let my personal experience as well as my research challenge your traditional perceptions. See if any part resonates with your heart in a way that gives you further comfort and peace. If it has, then I have achieved *my* life's purpose.

Introduction

Feeling Alone at Night?

What do you think about before you fall asleep at night? Are you at peace? Is falling asleep a natural transition into the abyss? Or do you, like most people, toss and turn as you struggle to allow yourself some much-needed rest?

Perhaps there's some unfinished business that comes to the forefront of your mind. It could be that woman from the office who's sending you mixed signals, or that guy you've been dating whose intentions remain a mystery. Perhaps the attractive woman who smiled at you in the elevator this morning has you weighing the risks of asking her out. Maybe the seemingly satisfied (and now sleeping) guy you've just had sex with has you wondering why you still feel so empty inside. And all these thoughts dancing around in your head carry within them the same core questions: What is love? Do I feel it? Is there something missing in the other person or is there just something wrong with me?

If your answers to those questions put your heart and mind at ease, a good night's sleep awaits you. If your answers miss the mark, you may have one of those sleepless nights.

So perhaps you put the television on and try to distract yourself, or start reading a book or magazine. Perhaps you just lose yourself in fantasies about being somewhere else or with someone else. You imagine you're making love to someone special. You wonder if there is really anyone out there for you and more importantly, where you might find them. The club scene doesn't seem much fun unless you're high. And that online dating could be a little scary.

Why does it seem that other people are able to find that someone special? People all around you appear to have found themselves someone to love, someone they can trust without fear. Why not you? You're not just looking for someone to talk to or have sex with. You are looking for that special someone you can risk being naked with emotionally, someone you can tell your deepest, darkest secrets to, someone who really listens and cares. Someone who doesn't forget. Why does this have to be so hard to do?

In the movies, the pain ends when we finally meet that special other, the one who "completes us," the way Renee Zellweger completes Tom Cruise in *Jerry Maguire. Sleepless in Seattle*'s Tom Hanks flies across the country to meet his perfect companion, Meg Ryan, and the two fall deeply in love at first sight. As the closing credits scroll down the screen, we find ourselves convinced that the entire process of finding the perfect mate should only take about two hours, and we naturally wonder what is wrong with us, when in real life it takes much, much longer. We even question our faith in the notion that God truly has a plan for us, a plan that pairs each of us with another who is a perfect fit.

In reality, current statistics tell us that most relationships will fail. Sadly then, for most of us actually keeping that special someone in our lives once we have found them is often a short-lived experience at best. For many, it never happens at all. How then do we reconcile this rather harsh reality with the idealistic longing we find deep within our souls?

And as we consider that contradiction, more riddles emerge. If we accept that all souls are tied to each other and ultimately to God, then we should be calmed and reassured by this connection, especially as we drift off to sleep. Instead, we often feel most vulnerable and alone in those moments. There must be a purpose served by this sense of isolation. Perhaps there is wisdom waiting in the questions it inspires.

And the big questions continue to challenge us: If we accept that our souls retain their identity beyond death, that strange feeling of continued comfort and communication with a loved one who has passed begins to make perfect sense and opens up a whole world of possibilities. If we further accept that the soul "remembers," that special person we are looking for might just be someone we have shared a lifetime with before: our soul mate. With this knowledge, that otherwise inexplicable sense of comfort and familiarity we feel with a person we have only just met takes on a new perspective. Embracing these concepts may offer some sense of purpose to the experience of pain and joy in our lives. It may even confirm the role played by a higher power in the drama of life.

I have spent most of my own life pondering these same questions. As a psychotherapist and as a metaphysical researcher of all that is unknown, I have tried to help my clients find the same answers as well. This book attempts to provide the reader with a sampling of my findings in this special, spiritual journey we call life.

✒ **Chapter 1** ✒

When Did You Stop Trusting Others?

At the core of all anger is a need that is not being fulfilled.
—Marshall B. Rosenberg

For a child, life is full of meaning and excitement. Each new day brings new people and new situations to discover. I love to see and meet young children. They are almost always energetic and curious and can find gratification in the simple pleasures of life: a rock, a twig, even their own toes. I love the way they fearlessly make eye contact as I walk past them. I love the eagerness with which they encounter new people, even staring unabashedly until they get a response. And once acknowledged, they respond with a warm and engaging smile. This is usually followed by furious hand-waving, perhaps some impromptu peek-a-boo, or any number of other universally accepted ways to say hello to a new friend. Children understand instinctively that we are really all the same in spirit. They trust without reservation and they love without fear. They know that we are all one with the world.

Their parents, on the other hand, have been hurt. They wish to keep their children safe from the disappointment and betrayal they have already experienced. So out of love and genuine parental concern, they repeatedly remind their children not to talk to strangers and warn of the horrible things that may happen if they do. By the time a child has reached first or second grade, I can see their growing reluctance to make eye contact. The innocence of childhood begins to fade and the spontaneity of the human spirit is stifled. The child is learning to be afraid.

In adolescence, social consciousness reaches new heights. Teens too often obsess about their peers' feelings, expectations, and judgments. *Everyone* is potentially dangerous. Hopefully, they have a strong bond with a parent, sibling, or friend who helps them maintain a balanced outlook and peace of mind. Studies repeatedly prove that a child who has at least one person with whom they identify can psychologically overcome the most difficult social and environmental threats.[1]

However, most adolescents are extremely impacted by the attitudes and values of their peers. Boys are expected to be tall, strong, and handsome. They are often socially and sexually insecure, but to be accepted they must instead appear confident and aggressive. Girls are expected to be thin, shapely, and pretty in order to be considered desirable and popular. Sadly, a significant percentage of the adolescent girls I see in counseling have secretly confided to me that their physical appearance is more important to them than their physical health. This tragic attitude is further evidenced by the increasing number of young women who take pills and laxatives, or just starve themselves to try to emulate what has become the media's ideal desirable girl. They are learning to pass judgment. And they tend to judge themselves and each other most harshly.

What about fun and spontaneity? By their late teens, a great many young people find they cannot put their worries and self-consciousness aside without the help of alcohol and drugs. Music, television, and movies all reinforce this cultural norm. For some this becomes the pattern for their adult life, usually with tragic consequences. Those fortunate enough to maintain their sense of balance and self worth, however, manage to emerge from adolescence relatively unscathed. They make their transition into adulthood armed with the traditional expectations and ambitions for love and happiness they have been promised await them.

But that promise is not without conditions. It requires that they find their perfect companion and *settle down*. Finding that right one means they can finally put their worries aside. With that special person they can open up and confide their true feelings, safe in the belief that they are valued and loved. Once they do, it follows that all their needs will be met, all their hopes will be realized, and all their dreams will come true. And they all live happily ever after....

However, the sad reality is that very few people have really been taught how to have a long-lasting, loving relationship. Not everyone's parents are the best role models, any more than their parent's parents were. Let's face it, none of the three Rs stand for Relationship. The traditional educational community does not yet recognize the need for even the most basic course on human relations during those critical years between kindergarten and twelfth grade. Given the importance of our relationships in every single aspect of our lives, it stands to reason that a course in relating to each other would be as valuable a component of a well-rounded education as any in math, science, or history, perhaps even more so. Its absence from the traditional school curriculum often deceives us into thinking it will be easy and effortless.

So, despite being rather ill-prepared for the challenges ahead, people meet, fall in love and marry, filled with great hope and conviction that the love they share will be enough to overcome anything that life throws their way. Unfortunately, fewer than half of these couples will remain together in the long term, as their joyfully idealistic expectations are eventually replaced by disillusionment and disappointment. No one ever told them that a lasting relationship requires work.

In fact, maintaining such bliss requires real diligence with regard to remaining open, honest, and communicative. Contrary to popular notions, long-lasting relationships are not dependent on how much the couple has in common or how much they seem to agree with each other. Studies have shown that the most compatible couples are able to be honest and open about their inevitable differences. Couples who are able to communicate well without being defensive, and who are able to resolve and heal their conflicts are the couples whose marriages last the longest.[2]

Many couples lose sight of the importance of maintaining time and intimacy with each other. After all, the media has invested millions of dollars in ads designed to convince them that the one who has the most toys wins in terms of both happiness and success. No small wonder then that they often become so preoccupied with making money, and focused on accumulating an endless array of material possessions, that they leave little or no time to just talk to each other. Real success in a relationship begins with a shared history of trust. This trust is born from compassionate communication and mutual understanding about what's important and what's not.

As babies we are born with this basic wisdom. Before we learned to fear and judge each other, before we grew up and settled down, our ability to trust was instinctive and natural, as was our joy and contentment. To master these vital skills now, we as adults have to relearn and remember.

What Are Soul Mates?

*The people we are in relationship with are always a mirror,
reflecting our own beliefs, and simultaneously
we are mirrors reflecting their beliefs.
So relationship is one of the most powerful tools for growth.*

—Shakti Gawain

Most people believe that their best chance for attaining lifelong love and happiness begins with finding just the right companion, or soul mate. The dictionary defines a soul mate simply as "a person ideally suited to another as a close friend or romantic partner."[1]

In my practice, I have spent many hours discussing this subject at length with my clients. In my personal life, I keenly recall first meeting my wife when she was only fourteen years old, three years my junior. On the surface, at the wise old age of seventeen, I wouldn't have considered a serious relationship with such a young girl. But there was such a comfort, familiarity, and chemistry between us that it caught me completely by surprise. Though our relationship has gone through many serious challenges, we have continued to be lovers and best friends for over thirty-eight years. I believe that we *are* soul mates.

However, my professional experience has taught me that the concept is not always so simple and straightforward. Each of us in the span of our lifetime meets people for whom we almost instantly feel an inexplicable comfort, familiarity, or chemistry. Conversely, we may also encounter those with whom we feel an instant discomfort for no apparent reason. Is this curious sensation of emotional recognition actually evidence of a soul mate? Can we encounter more than one in a lifetime?

My training in psychotherapy has taught me to recognize certain clinically defined connections between people. Some can be attributed to transference, where one's own feelings are unconsciously redirected onto another. Others are clearly associations, where the connection comes from feelings or memories of similar experiences or individuals. But what if the emotional connection that is felt cannot be explained by one's unconscious feelings or an earlier life experience?

Years of contemplation, meditation, and research have helped me to expand on that simplistic dictionary definition of a soul mate. I am certain that we are each born into this world with many spiritual connections, souls with whom we have shared some life experience. While some of those souls remain on the other side during the course of our lifetime, others incarnate along with us. These souls are here to help us learn how to live, love, and grow, and we are here to help them do the same. Consider then that we are all spiritual classmates learning together in the same Earth school. And we each bring with us our memories of past shared experiences to the classroom.

Personally, I can identify all of the individuals who have made a profound difference in my life. Among these people, I know with whom I have had particularly strong connections or bonds. In deep meditation, I have actually *seen* these energetic connections. Professionally, I have witnessed this remarkable phenomenon as well. A great many clients have recounted their individual soul mate experiences to me, and together we have worked to discover the importance and significance of each emotional tie.

I have researched hundreds of articles and books by those who have gained international acclaim as experts on the subject. I have also studied personally with many of them, including, most notably, Carolyn Myss, Dr. Raymond Moody, James Van Praagh, and Doreen Virtue. They vary widely in background, education, and orientation, but collectively they have inspired me to develop some simple concepts of my own. For a moment, let us consider that God's wisdom is limitless and freely available to every soul who has ever or will ever walk on this earth. As you entertain the far-reaching implications of this idea, let your imagination explore the possibility of these ten powerful but simply stated concepts:

1.   All human beings have souls composed of energy that are inherently connected to a divine energy source.

2.   The two primary forces that motivate us can usually be separated into those that originate in a desire for love and those that are based on some type of fear, or feeling of lack.

3.   Love is the language of God. It opens, attracts, and unifies. It is that which instinctively draws us all together as one.

4.   Fear is the language of darkness. It exists to give meaning and contrast to all that is light. It constricts, separates, and alienates. In the darkness, there is the illusion that we are disconnected and alone.

5.   There exists a hierarchy of entities to assist us in meeting these challenges and finding happiness, including ascended masters, angels, spirit guides, and each other. After all, we are spiritually all one.

6.   As unique entities of a universal oneness, we retain free choice to enlist (or decline) the help of others on the earth as well as the other side in our search to recognize, develop, and validate our loving connections.

7.   The goal of life is to recognize and mobilize loving energy. Life is also meant to continue the evolution of the individual soul to become more godlike or one with God.

8.   As souls, we all meet in spiritual committees before we are born to discuss what kind of lessons we need to learn. We then choose our environments and our experiences accordingly.

9.   Our souls gain wisdom through the challenges of life

experience, some of which may actually be prescripted.

10. The challenges are formulated using a whole array of possibilities, including parental choice, karma, life scripts, archetypal roles, relationship dynamics, and specific life challenges.

When these concepts are added to the mix, a broader definition of soul mate emerges. While a soul mate may be one with whom we remember (and may even resume) a love relationship from a prior lifetime, the term can also describe souls who are in our lives simply to help us find a deeper meaning or purpose, or provide us with an opportunity to learn or teach an important lesson. The following chapter illustrates this point.

Bonnie Found Her Soul Mate – and Much More

The purpose of relationships is not happiness, but transformation.
—Andrew Schneider

Three years ago, a young woman suffering from depression was referred to me by her physician. Bonnie had gone to him complaining of a sudden loss of energy and many sleepless, tear-filled nights. A thorough physical examination found Bonnie to be in good health, so her doctor recommended she try Zoloft, an antidepressant. Bonnie knew she needed help, but was reluctant to take that kind of medication, so she asked if he knew someone she could talk to instead. Her doctor gave Bonnie my card.

I met with Bonnie weekly over the next two years. We began by examining her relationships on all levels: emotional, physical and spiritual. She was an attractive woman of twenty-seven who had always enjoyed the attention of men, but was somewhat cautious and even skeptical about their intentions. The three men she had dated seriously over the last several years since college had each appeared to be warm, sensitive, and sincere in the beginning, but over time most had proven to be rather difficult or self-centered when conflicts inevitably surfaced. This pattern of disappointment seemed at last to have been broken when she began her most recent relationship with Bryant.

Bonnie met Bryant at a friend's party. He was different. There was an instant familiarity when they were introduced. Halfway through the night, Bryant meandered over to Bonnie's side of the room and started up a conversation. Bonnie found him to be very good-looking, but more importantly, he had an intensely soulful look in his big, brown eyes. As he talked, she found herself captivated by them. The conversation seemed effortless, and before long Bonnie realized that she and Bryant had talked so much that they were the last two people to leave the party.

Bryant took her phone number before they parted for the night. As he would later confess to Bonnie, he too had experienced an instant attraction the moment he laid eyes on her. Bonnie was by no means the first woman with whom he had felt a strong physical attraction but with Bonnie, the attraction seemed to run much deeper. When he got home, he couldn't stop thinking about her. Speaking with Bonnie for just one night was so comfortable and easy, he told her it felt as if they had known each other for years.

Like Bonnie, Bryant had never had an experience quite like this before. By his own admission, he was normally very cool and casual when it came to dating, but Bonnie seemed to strike a chord deep inside of him. Ordinarily, Bryant always waited at least three days before dialing a new woman's number so as not to appear too anxious or desperate for a date, but he found he just couldn't wait to call Bonnie. The next day Bryant found himself dialing her number to find out when they could get together again. When Bonnie heard Bryant's voice on the other end of the telephone line, she was both surprised and delighted.

"No, it's not too soon to call," she said. "I'd love to see you again tomorrow night!"

In the weeks and months that followed, Bonnie and Bryant spent much of their time together and quickly grew very close. Bonnie fell deeply in love with him. During one of our early sessions, she described it to me: "It was a love I had never experienced before. We had lots of good times. We were always together. I even drifted away from my friends and hobbies because I never wanted to do anything without him. Whenever I was away from him, I would start to miss him right away."

At this point, concerned that Bonnie's preoccupation with Bryant was diminishing her attention to personal interests, I proceeded to explore the relationship on a deeper level to assess some of the underlying dynamics.

"Did you ever want to pursue something that just you alone were interested in?" I asked.

"No. I decided that if Bryant wasn't interested, then I would rather just be with him."

"But did you think you might be giving up a part of yourself in the process?"

"No. Not at all! I finally met my soul mate and just wanted to be with him all the time."

"So what happened?"

"I loved him so much I would have done anything for him. I wanted to be his wife. I wanted to have his children."

"And what about Bryant? How did he feel?"

"He said he felt the same way. We talked about it a lot. He told me he had never met anyone like me before. He said he never wanted to be without me."

"But didn't you say something earlier about him being with a lot of other women before you?" Bonnie had, on several occasions, described Bryant's surprise at the intensity of his feelings for her. His powerful feelings for Bonnie seemed to indicate a radical departure from his usual level of interest.

"Yes. Exactly! And that's why he was so amazed that it was different being with me. He couldn't quite explain it, but when I said that I thought we were soul mates, he told me that must be the reason he had felt so comfortable with me from the very first night. He said it was like we knew each other before."

"And then what happened?"

"After three years of dating, I was still waiting for him to pop the question."

"About marriage?"

"Yes. After all, we had talked about it in a general way off and on. But he seemed a little nervous about actually making the commitment."

"So what did you do?"

"I just kept waiting. I was very patient. After all, we were together most of the time. So it was like we were married already."

"And then?"

"And then I found out he had cheated on me!" Bonnie's eyes welled up with tears.

"I couldn't believe it. I was shocked. I didn't understand what went wrong. It didn't make any sense at all."

Bonnie sobbed for several minutes before we could continue. I decided not to interrupt her. The tears were painful, but they seemed to give some relief to her pent-up confusion and frustration.

"I tried to talk with him," she continued. "I kept asking him why he would betray my trust. He just said he didn't know (and) that he did love me, but that wasn't any explanation. So I kept asking him over and over again, 'How could you do that? I thought we were soul mates.' He just kept saying, 'Yeah, we were. Believe me, I do love you. I guess I just wasn't ready to get married.'"

Bonnie was so deeply hurt that she couldn't forgive him, particularly when he didn't say anything to reassure her that it would never happen again. In fact, Bryant started becoming very defensive and angry. Sometimes he wouldn't talk at all. For Bonnie, this was the last straw. She finally got so frustrated that she felt she had no choice but to give up the relationship. After this, she slowly became very depressed.

"We were so good together," she said in one session. "I just can't understand what went wrong. I can't stop thinking about it."

Bonnie looked up and gazed deeply into my eyes. Sadly, she blurted out, "Maybe I just wasn't good enough for him."

"What do you mean?"

"Well, maybe I bothered him too much. Or maybe I didn't look good enough. After all, he was a good-looking guy and he could have been with a lot of girls. Maybe I did something wrong which caused him to want to be with another girl."

"You didn't make Bryant do anything," I interrupted. "You are not responsible for the way he acted. He is responsible for himself."

"But what if I *really* did something wrong?"

"If Bryant did not like something you said or did, then it was his responsibility to tell you that openly and honestly. That is how a healthy relationship works. That is how you maintain trust in a relationship and how you try to work things out."

"You don't keep problems to yourself," I continued, "and then look outside of your relationship for solutions. You make every effort not to keep your feelings secret from the one you love. And if you make any mistakes, particularly big ones, you make every effort to come clean as soon as possible so that the relationship may be salvaged. Unfortunately, Bryant was not ready to commit himself to a long-term, trusting relationship."

"But I thought he was the *one.* I was ready to change my whole life to be with him. Everything I felt in my gut told me that this relationship was different; that Bryant was my soul mate."

"I agree. From everything you told me, I have no doubt you *were* soul mates. But you might also consider that you were both destined to meet each other for a different reason other than marriage."

"A different reason?"

"Yes. It seems that by meeting each other, you both were given the opportunity to learn an important lesson."

"A lesson?"

"Yes. You were able to discover the importance of balance in a loving relationship in order for you to grow. You loved Bryant in such a way that you lost sight of yourself in the process. You sacrificed your individual passions and pursuits in order to be with him. For the sake of being with him all the time, you gave up that dance class you so enjoyed and even put off registering for the art class you had been so eager to take. His likes and dislikes began to determine yours, even when it came to dear friends that once meant so much to you. You were starting to lose your individual identity in such a way that you became wholly dependent on someone else for all of your happiness. That imbalance created a relationship that was no longer healthy for either one of you. It was actually a type of codependence. It was not the kind of love that really lasts."

Bonnie sat dumbfounded as she let this insight sink in. "So you don't think it would have lasted anyway?"

"No, at least not in a healthy way. In a way, it was a blessing in disguise that the relationship ended sooner rather than later. You were very deeply hurt, but you would have been much more devastated and depressed if you had actually become Bryant's wife and perhaps even started a family with him before you discovered that he was not being truthful with you all along."

"But, what about Bryant? How was I *his* lesson?"

"I would speculate that his defensiveness was based on guilt and his fear of looking foolish. I would venture further to say that he continues to be confused and empty, and that he probably misses you very much. But until he deals with his pain and does some of his own soul-searching, he will continue to form a series of dysfunctional relationships. So his lesson may well be that of facing his fears, overcoming his defenses, and honestly assessing his own direction and purpose in life. It is a basic lesson most of us need to learn in order to gain wisdom of the soul and peace of mind."

"So you see," I said, "Bryant is really not a bad guy. He is just a lost soul and until he truly embraces the lessons his life experiences are attempting to teach him, he will continue to repeat the same mistakes over and over again."

I suggested that the same dynamic should be applied to Bonnie regarding her experience. Through this process of review and examination of a heartbreaking experience, she now had the opportunity to act on her newfound understanding of her own patterns of behavior. In recognizing her tendency to surrender herself to a relationship, she could now choose to focus on maintaining a healthy balance between her own needs and her partner's, and in doing so drastically improve her chances for a successful, loving relationship in the future.

Bonnie listened intently as this new perspective emerged. Her sad and painful experience suddenly took on increased meaning and purpose. She took a long, deep breath and sat back in her chair. "Oh, now I get it! It's all starting to make sense. In fact, I'm suddenly starting to feel much better. What a relief!"

"Soul-searching and psychotherapy are at first very scary and disturbing to one's ego," I said. "But now you can see that the relatively short period of discomfort is well worth the life-long wisdom that is gained."

I went on to explain that though Bryant may have indeed been a real soul mate, the relationship with him was not necessarily her one and only chance for life-long happiness. Though a soul mate you encounter may have shared past life or between-life experiences with you, their current role may not be one of life-long companionship and love. Some may come into our lives to give us an opportunity for growth or deeper understanding. Some connect with us solely to facilitate their own life lessons. Life-long relationships may be developed with *any* kindred spirit. After all, we are really all connected with each other, as well as with the Divine.

"So you may well encounter other soul mates along your life path," I said, "either to learn another lesson or maybe just to gain more soul growth *without* any emotional pain."

"I should be so lucky," Bonnie laughed.

I continued to meet with Bonnie for the next five months. Once she was finally able to make sense of the most difficult period in her life, Bonnie gradually began feeling much more relaxed and happy. Her clearer understanding of what had happened with Bryant ultimately gave her the confidence to move past this great hurt, so much so that she began to think seriously about dating again.

About four months after our sessions ended, Bonnie called me to say that she had recently met someone who was "even better than Bryant ever was."

"Really?" I asked.

"Yeah, really. He's a great guy! We hit it off right away and I got that same gut feeling again. But this guy told me that he had had his own problems a few years ago and he wasn't afraid to go talk to someone in order to work it out. In fact, we both have dated similar kinds of people—in the sense that they would get very defensive when you tried to talk about certain things. But now *we* can talk about anything! We have faith, not fear, about the future of our relationship."

"I'm very happy for you," I responded. "I appreciate your call. It's always nice to hear when people are happy and doing well." I hung up the phone feeling delighted for Bonnie and the wisdom she had attained.

Soul-Searching: Meditation Can Be the First Step

Any fool can run towards the light. It takes a master with courage to turn and face the darkness and shine his own light there.

—Leslie Fieger

To say that most people's daily lives are very busy is an understatement. Once the alarm clock rings in the morning, you rush out of bed, make yourself some coffee, take a shower, get the kids ready for school, and eventually leave for work yourself. On the train or in your car, you are bombarded with music, talk radio, or the news. Then you have a full day of work.

When you return home, you may have to worry whether your children have after-school activities or homework and prepare a big dinner. Perhaps you are able to have some conversation around the dinner table before the meal ends and you have to start the after-dinner chores. Once that is done, it's time to help your children with more homework, showers, and bedtime. Then perhaps you are able to watch a little television before you start thinking about what you have to do for yourself before you pass out at the end of the night.

Where in all of this is the quality of life? When can you unwind? Do you wait until Saturday each week before you can give yourself permission to relax, or are even your weekends consumed by more "must-do" activities like grocery shopping or laundry? Once again, I ask, "Where is the *quality* of life?"

Clients make appointments at my office to talk about exactly this issue. They stop all the busy-ness of each day to step into the quiet sanctuary within the four walls of my office. Once they step inside, they often find immediate relief in the awareness that they have temporarily escaped the self-imposed treadmill of life. Once inside this room, clients instinctively turn off their cell phones, sit in a relaxed position, and begin to take nice deep breaths.

I purposely set aside a few moments at the beginning of each session to let each client quietly settle in and gain his or her composure. I already sense whether the week has been more difficult or forgiving than usual. For example, I usually ask John, who is one of my clients, to take a few moments, lean back, relax his shoulders and legs, and start the session whenever he is ready.

Sometimes, John can't get comfortable at all. A week's worth of stress has taken its toll.

"I can't relax," he responds. "It's been a terrible week. I'm running all day and when it's eleven o'clock and I'm finally done with what I want to do for the day, I lay down but my mind keeps racing. It's only when I've had a particularly exhausting day that I'm able to fall asleep once my head hits the pillow."

Like John, most people look forward to a counseling session because it's really an appointment with their inner self. In the peace and quiet, they are able to begin reflecting on life and the reasons they are feeling what they are feeling. Most of us are a lot like John, having never really experienced a full hour of time when our minds aren't reviewing a Rolodex of information in anticipation of the next worry or some unfinished task.

But our minds hunger for a break from this hectic routine. None of us should have to go so far as to make a professional appointment to indulge our need to pause and reflect. Our minds will automatically slow down and rest if we just let them. Take your lunch on a park bench or a local beach instead of a noisy cafeteria and you'll notice how quickly and naturally your mind downshifts into a zone of tranquility.

A better example is when you are sitting at home at night and you find yourself captivated by a gently flickering candle, or the

dancing flames in a fireplace. Effortlessly, the mind ι
as a simple focal point. Automatically, the light sooth
and mesmerizes one's consciousness, capturing its ε
it does this, all the constant chatter that routinely interreres with
one's focus starts to dissipate and then fades away. This process
is an example of the mind's natural desire to seek the peace and
comfort of meditation.

But you don't have to wait until you're lying on a beach or
staring at a flame to find this natural tranquilizer. A meditative
state can be easily achieved within fifteen minutes in the comfort
of your home, at any time. Once you allow your mind to find
solace and peace, you may find that it is no longer important to
find distractions or waste your time and energy on trivial and/
or negative issues. Instead, you may find that your soul prefers to
focus on the more integral aspects of your quality of life. You may
more easily identify the harmonious or conflicted areas of your life,
both with others and within yourself. You may finally give yourself
permission to spend your days in gratitude, appreciation, and love
rather than preoccupied with fears and defenses. Once you begin
to quiet your mind, you can start that soul-searching that helps you
find yourself. Once you feel more together inside, you are more
likely to find a healthy relationship on the outside with another
person. You may even be able to better recognize that soul mate
you would like to have in your life forever.

Do you have fifteen or twenty minutes today? Here is a simple
relaxation technique that will help you quiet the noise of the day
and relax. This can also be your first step on the journey to your
deeper self:

1. Find a spot that is fairly quiet and free from the usual
    distractions: television, radio, computer, or telephone.
2. Sit in a comfortable position with your legs uncrossed and
    feet flat on the floor.
3. Close your eyes and set your intention on taking slow,

deep breaths.

4. Slowly chant a pleasing sound or word with each breath. This word, called a mantra, can be any word or sound that you associate with love, comfort, or oneness. It could also be a simple, pleasing sound like *om*, which is considered the universal mantra.

5. As an alternative to using a mantra, you may choose a progressive muscle relaxation technique. Initially developed by Herbert Benson, M.D., it has also been called the relaxation response. Simply focus your intention on progressively relaxing each group of muscles in your body, starting from the top of your head and working down methodically to the tips of your toes. You may be surprised how, in a matter of minutes, you can achieve a state of relaxation you had never thought possible.

My first introduction to the power of meditation occurred when I was a college freshman in the early '70s, during my first year living away from home. As an avid fan of The Beatles, I marveled at their massive success in music. When even their international fame and great wealth left each of them confused and unhappy, I followed their personal transformations as they struggled to find answers. Their well-publicized soul-searching experiences introduced the western world to Transcendental Meditation as they traveled to India to meet and study with the Maharishi Mahesh Yogi, its founder.

As an eighteen-year-old who fled a rather tumultuous family environment by running off to college, I found their quest for inner peace and enlightenment fascinating and inspiring. When the opportunity arose on campus to learn the same type of meditation, I felt compelled to investigate further. I attended an introductory seminar and learned that there was scientific evidence that one becomes measurably relaxed while practicing meditation. In fact, meditating so relaxes the mind and body that the respiration and heart rates drop even lower than they do during deepest sleep.[2] When the seminar was over, I was ready to sign up.

After paying an affiliated teacher a fee, I attended a small, sweet, initiation ceremony and was given a special mantra to chant out loud, and then later to myself. I was told that the mind enjoyed the simplicity of this word, and it would be naturally attracted to focus on it. I did not need to concentrate; the only need was to contemplate the sound of the word, since no effort was involved. I was not to worry if at any time my mind drifted away from the sound because it would gradually drift back again. In the process, all other thoughts would fade away.

I began meditating for fifteen to twenty minutes before breakfast and dinner each day. It was deeply relaxing and thoroughly enjoyable. I was amazed at the way both my mind and my muscles would simultaneously release a tremendous amount of tension. What I had always thought to be my own normal level of alertness now seemed more like an uncomfortable sense of hypervigilance and anticipation. After only one week of daily meditation, my *new* normal was to feel relaxed most of the time.

After two weeks, my meditations became even easier and more pleasing. As soon as I closed my eyes, my mind seemed eager to return to its relaxed state. The only thought that would remain was the simple sound of my mantra. Soon afterward, I even experienced blocks of time during my meditation when the sound of my mantra disappeared as well. I was fully awake but I had no thoughts at all. All that remained was a warm, euphoric sensation of simply being conscious and alive. It was the best sensation I had ever experienced in my eighteen years. Soon my twenty minutes would pass, and once again I naturally returned to the pace of my normal activities.

As a quiet, introspective teenager, my meditations greatly enhanced the inner dialogue of my thought process. I found that I became more focused and aware in my daily life, and there was much less noise and chatter in my head. I had always been the kind of person who would instinctively contemplate my place in the world, but my new meditative experience helped me to gain more clarity in my soul-searching. I quickly became aware of those situations that caused me stress, and I automatically started steering clear of them. I learned what type of interactions with people disturbed me, and I learned to quickly evaluate whether my conversations with them were worthwhile. There were smaller but no less significant revelations as well. One day for example, while standing in a ticket line for a horror movie, I found myself wondering why I would want to pay money for an experience designed solely to induce anxiety and fear under the guise of entertainment. I chose to get out of that line and seek a better way to find excitement on a Saturday night.

I didn't know at the time that I would revisit my earliest roots of contemplation and analysis years later in my career as a psychotherapist. Even after many years of experience, I am still learning about life as much from the inside as I do from the outside. I am also helping others to do the same.

Soul Mates: The Love Never Dies

Love is patient; love is kind…
In a word, there are three things that last forever:
faith, hope, and love; but the greatest of them all is love.

—1 Corinthians 13:4

S asha and Dale first came to me for couples counseling about twenty years ago, and I had seen Sasha privately on and off in the years that followed. A vivacious and energetic woman now in her early sixties, Sasha came back to see me after her husband Dale was diagnosed with lung cancer. The harsh reality of Dale's health issues had pushed their already strained relationship into crisis, and Sasha described Dale's refusal to speak openly about it as a constant source of sadness and frustration for her. Like many couples that have been together for decades, she and Dale had developed a pattern of responding to problems that fell sadly short of the mark when it came to actual resolution. If they were to deal with something of this magnitude, Sasha knew they needed to find a better way to communicate.

Sasha met and married her soul mate Dale almost forty years ago. They had two grown children, now in their thirties who had children of their own.

In the course of their marriage, Sasha and Dale had weathered their share of the usual trials and tribulations. With each conflict, feelings were hurt, anger flared and sometimes periods of silence followed. In that silence—which Sasha said could often last for days on end—they would completely withdraw from each other. Staring into space and wondering what went wrong, each would try and make sense of the thoughts and feelings that the conflict provoked.

As I had observed in their couples sessions years before, rehashing the endless details—looking for who was right and who was wrong—became frustrating and cumbersome for both Sasha and Dale. This pattern of nonproductive silence gradually evolved into a benign indifference for the tedious details of any conflict. Each invariably shifted their focus to the outside world; the sun through the trees and the clouds in the sky always seemed to help them rearrange their priorities. In this solitude, each seemed to return to the understanding that life is too short to spend much time on the small stuff. Individually reflecting on their relationship as a whole—recalling how they met, remembering the good times with family and friends, as well as the tender intimacy they shared— both of them came to reaffirm their connection as lifelong lovers and special soul mates.

Based on these periods of introspection, Sasha and Dale came to the separate conclusions that it was time to reconnect with each other. Inevitably it seemed each would decide that whatever it was that they were fighting about wasn't so important after all. Their eyes would meet and carry the important message of the other's readiness for reconciliation, and without words peace was finally restored.

Now as they faced the devastating news of Dale's cancer, Sasha and Dale appeared to have reached a point in their relationship where they could not nonverbally resolve their conflicts anymore. A simple glance was not enough to prompt communication and reconnection. Dale was unable to bring himself to talk openly about his illness. It was the biggest problem they had ever encountered.

"I can't take it anymore," declared Sasha in one session, as the tears filled her eyes. "He never wants to talk about it. We can talk about the doctor's appointments. We can talk about the chemotherapy. And we talk a lot about all the medical bills. But he never tells me how he really feels."

"So what are the doctors saying about his prognosis?" I asked.

"Well, they never give me a straight answer, but it's pretty clear he's getting worse," Sasha continued.

"And what are they telling Dale?"

"He doesn't even ask." replied Sasha. "He leaves it up to me to get all the information."

"Really?"

"Well, he's always been that way. We've been married almost forty years, and he's usually been the quiet type. But there's so much to talk about now."

"That's for sure."

"I was planning to retire next year and we were going to travel. Now with him getting sicker and the bills getting bigger, I don't know what we are going to do!" Sasha started to cry. "I'm so depressed and I'm so frustrated with him. I cry every day now."

"What does he say when you start to cry?" I asked.

"He just shakes his head and goes to another room. Then he picks up the paper or turns on the TV."

"So he can't deal with any of it," I commented.

"No, not at all."

"Rather than letting him off the hook, what if you follow him into the other room and tell him you need his help with your retirement plans and all of the financial decisions?"

"I've tried that," Sasha explained, "but he says he can't talk to me when I'm so emotional."

"Of course you're *so emotional*," I replied. "It's a very difficult situation and you need to talk to someone."

"Well he's always accused me of being too sensitive, even before this all happened. He always tells me that if I would just find more things to do I wouldn't have the time to dwell on all of the problems."

"Apparently, this is how he has learned to cope with *his* problems," I said. "However, I think it's unfair, at least in this situation, to say that you are dwelling on the problem. It seems in fact that *you* are the only one dealing with the problem. If he were able to share some of the burden of these problems, particularly the medical issues and his own prognosis, it is likely that you wouldn't be so overwhelmed and emotional."

"Yes, I get so frustrated. It drives me nuts."

"So when you're at your wits end, what does he say?"

"Now you're *really* out of control. You better go see a shrink!"

Historically, Sasha had no idea what she should expect in a healthy marital relationship. Certainly, by her own description, Sasha's parents' relationship was far from ideal. Her father was rather unemotional and demanding and her mother seemed resigned to suffer in silence. The kind of relationship Dale suggested for the two of them often fell short of her emotional needs. But the truth is, the discrepancy between what is idealized and/or expected from a relationship and what actually takes place is *every* couple's issue. Because of this I felt that Sasha was a good candidate for group therapy.

The particular group I had in mind for Sasha was one I had conducted for some time, made up of both men and women who routinely and candidly discuss the conflicts in their relationships. I act as the moderator and facilitator for the group, but it is the interaction of the participants in the group that provides the powerful support dynamic I felt would be especially beneficial to Sasha.

In the group, Sasha was pleasantly surprised to find that the conversations she often held silently in her head could be discussed openly, in detail. Sasha was particularly impressed with the men in the group. They were able to talk about emotional topics as easily as the women. Sometimes, they even cried. Suddenly, Sasha no longer felt "overly sensitive" or "crazy" as Dale had so often described her recent reactions. In fact, she felt very normal.

Sasha was able to use her new support network to her best advantage. When problems became overwhelming, Sasha would continue to seek Dale's involvement. Sometimes he responded, but if Sasha got "too emotional," then he would again return to his own habits and retreat. That's when Sasha would see that it was actually Dale who was overwhelmed with emotion. After all, it was he who was dying and it was he who couldn't bear dealing with it. So instead of getting frustrated and upset, Sasha would pick up the phone and talk to a group member for support. (In this particular group, it was understood that getting emergency support between meetings was permissible.)

Sometime later, Sasha shared a story with the group regarding the impact that their support had had on the difficulties she and Dale were experiencing. She described an evening earlier that week when she had again attempted to talk to Dale about how she was feeling. This time when Dale retreated to the den to escape the emotional exchange, she did not follow him as she had done in the past. Instead, she went to the kitchen and picked up the phone. She didn't return for an hour.

"Where were you?" he asked when Sasha finally came into the den.

"In the kitchen, on the phone," replied Sasha.

"For an hour?"

"Yes."

"Who were you talking to for so long?"

"Someone from group."

"Someone from group? What were you talking about for so long?"

"About me. About me and you. About this whole situation."

"Hmm," Dale commented and paused. "And *what* about the whole situation?"

"Do you really want to know?" Sasha asked, her eyebrows raised.

"Well, if you can tell someone from group, I guess you can tell me." Dale replied.

"Well, I was upset and I didn't want to bother you with it," Sasha explained.

"Oh, don't worry. I can handle it." Dale replied.

The other group members sat in silent support as Sasha continued relating the exchange: She had talked and Dale had listened. She talked about their history together and all the good times they had shared over the past forty years. She also talked about her fears about Dale's current condition.

"You know the cancer is spreading," Sasha told him cautiously, waiting for his reaction.

Dale sat motionless, staring into the distance.

"The doctors said that there is no sense trying another round of chemotherapy," Sasha continued.

"Yes, I thought that's what they were trying to say," acknowledged Dale, speaking very softly.

"I'm afraid. I don't know what I am going to do." Tears welled up in Sasha's eyes. Then one rolled down her cheek.

Dale quickly looked away and then he looked down toward the floor, as Sasha swallowed hard and tried to hold back her tears. At that point, Dale seemed unable to contain himself any longer. "I don't know what I'm going to do either!" he burst out, sobbing uncontrollably.

Sasha instinctively went over to Dale and held him tightly to her bosom. Dale continued to cry for what seemed like an eternity.

"I'm sorry," Dale blurted out.

"Sorry? For what?" asked Sasha.

"I've always been the strong one. I thought that if I broke down, you would really be a mess."

"No! Not at all! I've been having such a hard time because I didn't have you to talk to, which made me feel lonely and crazy."

"Are you sure you're okay? You're not angry with me?" Dale persisted in disbelief.

"No. I just want you to be open and honest with me about how you really feel."

Sasha paused to reflect. "You know, when we were younger, one of the things I loved about you was that you were honest and to the point. I never had to wonder what was wrong."

"Yeah. You're right," Dale replied.

"However, you always had a hard time saying that you loved me," Sasha added with a smirk.

"Why should I have to say it? If I didn't love you, why would I be with you for forty years? I always said that actions speak louder than words," Dale added.

"Well, it's nice to hear it anyway." Sasha persisted. "After all, it's not asking for a lot."

Dale paused and took a deep breath. "Listen, I have to say I really appreciate all you've done for me lately: Going with me to all the doctor's appointments, taking care of all the phone calls, keeping track of all the bills…and you do it all without me having to ask you! That's really sweet. I don't know what I would do if you weren't here."

"Thank you, honey. It's nice to know that I'm appreciated," Sasha said with a smile, giving Dale another big hug.

"You know I really do love you, don't you?" asked Dale.

"Yes, I know," replied Sasha. "And I love you too, with all my heart."

Sasha described that conversation as a turning point in the relationship, one that brought them to a new, deeper, spiritual level. In a later session she confided to the group that she and Dale had finally begun talking about all the really important issues regarding his medical condition.

"If I get really bad, I want you to promise me that you won't let them hook me up to all of those machines. I'd rather just die peacefully at home."

"I promise," said Sasha reassuringly.

Over the next six months, Sasha continued to care for Dale as his condition gradually grew worse. It was a difficult struggle, but with only occasional setbacks, Sasha and Dale were finally able to share the burden of his illness. Sasha was also grateful that she had the full attention and support of her group to help her throughout the ordeal. Dale had become increasingly fragile, his skin had a gray pallor and his speech had grown labored and weak. One afternoon while watching television, he passed out on the couch.

When Dale didn't respond to her voice, Sasha grabbed the phone and called an ambulance. She held his face next to hers, feeling his shallow and labored breathing as they waited for what seemed like an eternity until the ambulance arrived. The ambulance rushed the barely conscious Dale to the hospital with Sasha still at his side.

In the emergency room Dale seemed stable, but weak. He was admitted to the intensive care unit and Sasha remained by his side until an oncology specialist could be located. Hours later, a specialist was able to conduct a brief assessment of Dale's condition. Though Dale remained unresponsive, Sasha sat at his bedside cradling his hand in hers. Standing at the foot of Dale's bed, his eyes darting from the chart to Sasha and back again, the physician tried to be optimistic.

"Your husband seems to be in a semi-comatose state. We'll have to run some tests and keep him here for awhile under observation." His eyes diverted to Dale's chart again.

"And then what?" Sasha interjected, feeling very panicky.

"Well, we'll have to see. In the meantime, we'll treat him with some medication in an IV. We'll keep him in the oxygen tent and we can feed him through a tube. That should help."

As the doctor spoke these words, Sasha saw Dale's entire body suddenly become agitated. He seemed to be experiencing some type of convulsion. Sasha screamed and the ICU nurse hurried her out of Dale's room as the doctor prepared to administer medication.

"Is he going to be alright?" Sasha asked the nurse.

"Yes, I'm sure he'll be okay," replied the nurse reassuringly. "I'm sure the doctor will do everything possible to keep your husband out of danger."

"Okay," Sasha replied hopefully as the nurse led her to a seat in the waiting area.

Ten, twenty, then thirty minutes passed before the doctor came out to report on Dale's condition. When the doctor finally reappeared, Sasha leapt from her seat. He looked directly into Sasha's eyes and said, "I'm sorry. We did everything we could, but the cancer had spread too far." Sasha slumped back into the waiting room couch, covered her face with her hands and wept. Despite Dale's months of decline, his death suddenly seemed so abrupt. They had both known this was coming, but the end still came as a brutal shock.

"I keep thinking that there was something more I could have done," Sasha said in one of the group sessions shortly after Dale's death. The group had become a great source of comfort and encouragement for her over the course of Dale's illness. This was especially true now as she dealt with the grief of this enormous loss.

"No, you did everything physically possible," one member reassured her.

"You were also his emotional support to the very end," said another. "He told you himself that he didn't know how he could have gotten through it without you."

The following week, Sasha again seemed agitated. Sensing the tension, a group member asked, "Are you okay, Sasha?"

Sasha broke down in tears. "I haven't been able to sleep all week. I keep thinking that Dale is angry with me."

"Angry with you?" I asked. "Why would he be angry with you?"

"I started thinking about that last night in the hospital. The doctor was talking about keeping Dale in intensive care and having him hooked up to all kinds of wires and tubes and machines, and I didn't say anything to stop them!"

"But the doctor was just talking about what could be done," a member interjected.

"But that's when Dale started having convulsions," Sasha retorted. "They say people can still hear things when they're unconscious. I think that when I didn't say anything to protect him, he got agitated and *that's* why he died!"

"Are you saying that somehow he died because of you?" I asked.

"Yes, maybe that's what happened. That's what I've been thinking about all week." Sasha began to sob again.

"No, that's ridiculous!" exclaimed another group member. "You loved him very much and you would have never done anything to hurt him. We know that and he knows that."

"How do you know he knows that?" Sasha challenged.

"Because I'm sure his spirit is right here in this room and I'm sure he knows very well all you tried to do for him," the member said.

"But how do you know?" Sasha persisted. "I've been praying all week for some kind of sign and I haven't seen anything. I don't know what to think. I'd like to think you are all right in what you're saying, but I just can't help thinking that I might have done something wrong."

"No, you did as much as you could," declared another member. "You definitely did much more than I would have done in your situation. In fact, you always put *his* needs before your own. You're amazing. And he just started to realize it toward the end."

"That helps me feel better," responded Sasha. "Maybe I'll be able to get some sleep tonight."

"I hope so," added another participant. "You're a wonderful woman and you have nothing to feel guilty about."

"Thank you," responded Sasha gratefully, "but I still wish he would give me some kind of sign that he's okay." Her eyes glanced upward.

A few days after the group therapy session, my wife and I had plans to attend a small seminar featuring Judy Guggenheim, the author of *Hello from Heaven!* Her book is a fascinating collection of 350 accounts of after-death communications, or ADCs. These communications, sometimes received though a medium and sometimes occurring spontaneously, are fascinating examples of the enduring nature of the soul and the incredible power of love to transcend death. Having read Ms. Guggenheim's book a few years earlier and having had several ADC experiences myself, I was eager to hear her speak.

The opening presenter was a psychic who would be talking about her personal experiences with the spiritual world. Since my nephew's wife, Marianne, had recently lost her father, I suggested to my wife that we ask them to attend the seminar with us. I hoped that Marianne would be able to get a quick reading from this psychic and possibly hear from her father.

When we got to the meeting, I was glad to see that there were only about twenty-five people in attendance, so the chance of getting a reading would be good.

The psychic, as expected, gave a wonderful presentation and then offered to circulate around the audience to see if any messages came through from the other side. As the woman approached our group, we all gazed at her intently. I was hoping that my niece would be able to get some kind of message from her father. My niece and the psychic's eyes met, but then she turned away, looking first at my nephew, my wife, and then at me. Her eyes lingered on mine.

"I have a message for you," she stated emphatically.

"Okay," I responded, nodding my head.

"There's a male spirit in the room with us," she continued.

"Do you have a name?" I asked.

The psychic paused, appearing to be tuning into a voice inside of her head. "I think it starts with a *D*. Oh, here it is: *Dale* is the name I'm getting."

Then she looked at me and asked, "Do you know anyone named Dale?"

"Yes," I immediately replied, realizing that out of the hundreds of people I knew, I only knew one person named Dale: Sasha's husband.

"Well, he wants to say hello to you and let you know that he is okay." She paused for a moment to tune-in for anything more.

"No, that's all I'm getting," she said. "Now he's gone." She looked up at me again. "Is this person related to you?" she asked.

"No," I replied. "Not to me."

"Well, then you are supposed to relay this message to the person Dale is related to," she concluded.

"Oh, I will." I responded. "I definitely will."

When it was time for group therapy the following week, Sasha entered the office. She still appeared to be upset. The group took a few moments to settle down and soon all eyes were focused on Sasha.

"What's new since last week?" I asked.

"I'm trying hard not to feel guilty," she responded. "Some days are good and then there are other days when I just can't stop thinking about it, particularly at night, when I'm all alone in bed. I just keep replaying that last day over and over again. I keep seeing how Dale was so disturbed that last day in the hospital. I just keep praying every night for some kind of sign that he's okay."

"Well, I have to tell you something," I stated intently. "I attended a seminar this past week and I saw a psychic there who talked about her experiences. Of course, you all know I don't believe there is any such thing as a coincidence. Well, I was able to get a brief reading, but the reading wasn't about me: It was about you."

Sasha continued to sit, motionless, her eyes fixed on mine.

"The only thing the psychic told me was to give you one simple message: Dale says hello and he's okay."

Sasha started to cry. "I can't believe I finally got my sign. That's what I've been praying for all week. Thank you!"

"No, don't thank me," I responded. "Whatever happened is way beyond my control. I just *happened* to go to a meeting." I continued, "I hope you now realize that Dale is in a place where he knows how much you loved him all of these years. If there was any confusion at the end of his life, he knows why and he knows better now. The love you shared never ends. Once you make that kind of connection with anyone in any lifetime, the love is eternal. Real love never dies."

Sasha continued to participate in group therapy for about a year after Dale's passing. Over time she was able to better embrace and understand the journey they had shared, strengthened by her belief that she and Dale were indeed soul mates and secure in the knowledge that their love continues to endure.

Tragedy Provokes Spiritual Inquiry

*The period of greatest gain in knowledge and experience
is the most difficult period in one's life.*

—Dalai Lama

The death of a loved one is probably the most difficult experience of one's life. Whether it is the loss of a parent, spouse, sibling, or a child, the pain invariably strikes us very deep. At times like these, the business of life abruptly stops and we are forced to pause and reflect on what life is really all about. Once again, in quiet prayer or meditation, we may conclude that the importance of one's lifetime can be measured simply by how often we give love and how deeply we are loved. Love is what we hope for. Love is what we search and live for. Love is what connects us all.

Love is so important and so powerful that we dwell on the spirit and energy of love when someone we love dies. But there is a vast amount of research that suggests that the spirit and communication of love is stronger than the physical body.[1] The body may get sick, deteriorate, and ultimately cease to function, but love's connection is soul-to-soul and this love never dies.

We know instinctively that love transcends life because it lives in our hearts and minds forever. But since we live on an earthly plane, we like to have that fact validated by our five senses as well. So it is natural to fantasize or imagine that we may see our loved ones, hear their voices, or even feel their caresses. On many occasions, however, I have found the contact is quite real.

In my office, more than half of my clients report some form of

ADC following the death of a beloved spouse or family member. Many other therapists and researchers have had similar findings. Early in my career as a therapist, I wondered why this fact was not well known to most professionals. In discussing this issue with my clients, it became apparent that most people had not reported these events to therapists or other professionals simply because no one ever asked.

Traditional psychotherapists and medical doctors are not taught to integrate spirituality into their work with patients during their traditional schooling. As a result, spirituality is often thought of as being best left in a separate category. Unless the physician has opted to take special coursework on the psychological treatment regarding death and dying, questions related to a patient's experiences with the paranormal are most likely overlooked. However, based on my clinical experiences, asking a client about his or her interactions with the spiritual realm—in both waking and sleep states—is always a rich source of what is deeply meaningful to each person. I find that asking such questions almost always leads to valuable discussions of the deep, profound spiritual values and conflicts they are often otherwise reluctant to share.

When the author Judy Guggenheim and her former husband Bill posed the question to the public, "Have you been contacted by someone who has died?" they received over 3,300 firsthand responses.

Dr. Raymond A. Moody, MD, PhD reported in his book *Reunions* that sixty-six percent of widows have had ADC contacts with their deceased husbands. Even a greater percentage (seventy-eight percent) of parents reported some form of contact by their recently deceased children.[2]

With a PhD in philosophy, Moody is an expert in Greek mythology and cultural practices. In a presentation entitled "Soul Survival," Moody recounted the ancient writings of Herodotus concerning the old Greek legend of the *psychomanteum*. According to legend, the psychomanteum was a complex underground institution located in the ancient city of Ephyra in Epirus, an area in western Greece, designed for the explicit purpose of making contact with loved ones after death. Remarkably, in the late 1950s, the remains of an actual site fitting the legend's description were discovered by a Greek archaeologist named Sotiris Dakaris.

Moody visited and studied the site himself. Based on his findings there, he went on to postulate that the critical element of contact involved an old, almost lost art of mirror gazing. In repeated tests using a dim light, a long and focused meditative gaze, and a strong, conscious intention to make contact, Moody found that a mirror could facilitate the reflection of images of loved ones long gone. In fact, in fifty percent of the cases, complex communications took place as well!

If you are feeling adventurous, mirror gazing is quite simple to attempt on your own. Sit comfortably in a darkened room in front of a mirror and position a very dim light (a nightlight will do nicely) behind you in such a way that it is not reflected in the mirror. With a relaxed, slightly unfocused gaze, stare into your own eyes. As you continue this gaze, maintain the intent that you seek to contact a loved one who has passed on. You may find that other images will appear in the mirror with you, or that your own image alters. These are likely manifestations of the souls that are close to you. When mirror gazing is approached with a calm curiosity, the experience can be quite profound and enjoyed without fear.

There are hundreds upon hundreds of books, articles, and scientific inquiries about paranormal experiences spanning hundreds and hundreds of years. Recently, however, the mainstream media has realized the general public's hunger for such information, as evidenced by the popularity of such programs as John Edward's *Crossing Over*, where he offers communication as a medium with deceased loved ones for the studio audience; or *America's Best Psychic*, where individuals with psychic abilities are tested and showcased in a contest format.

But the realm of the spiritual is not something you *observe*, it's something you *engage*. As noted earlier in this book, the direct connection with all that is spiritual requires first that we disconnect from the outside clutter of daily life through meditation or other relaxation techniques. However advanced modern man has become in terms of technology and world communications, sadly, much of our spiritual knowledge has been abandoned or forgotten. Perhaps the time has come to rediscover that ancient wisdom.

Our need to ask the most compelling spiritual questions comes most often when we are faced with hardship, but the deepest, soul-searching questions arise from tragedy and loss. There are many ways to redirect our conscious awareness to discover the treasures of wisdom hidden inside each of us. The ancients found herbs and roots that would induce psychotropic states in which they believed they could communicate with their gods. Even today, there are many indigenous tribal groups that use herbal-assisted ceremonies to seek altered states of mind. In the 1960s, Timothy Leary thought that ingesting LSD was the quickest way to "tune-in and turn-on" that inner communication. But I certainly do not recommend these artificial chemical inducements as a means of gaining profound spiritual insights.

Despite our modern culture's temptation to take a magic pill anytime we want to change our mood or consciousness, there are completely natural, drug-free techniques that can take us anywhere we want to go. In fact, these altered states of consciousness can be achieved naturally on a daily basis through many forms of meditation, visualization, or self-hypnosis. As discussed earlier, by simply allowing your attention to be captured while gazing at a fish tank, enjoying a quiet breeze in the park, or the sun on your skin at the beach, you can accomplish the same state. In each case, as you relax, your thoughts naturally dissipate and you are left thinking about nothing at all. This is an altered state of consciousness that opens your mind to those deeper questions and provides a connection to the source of the answers.

A wake or burial ceremony is an event where we traditionally acknowledge the impact of death. We mourn the loss of a loved one and the void their absence creates in our lives. We draw upon memories of our shared experiences and feelings we had for them. We become acutely aware of the preciousness and fragility of life, but we also contemplate our own mortality. Death forces us to think about what our own lives mean and compels us to reevaluate our priorities. Culturally we have established traditions surrounding death that encourage us to set aside this time for reflection.

Science tells us we use a mere five percent of our brain's capacity in our normal day-to-day living. The blessing of tragedy is that it provokes us to use more of that capacity to ponder the deepest of questions. In the darkness of grief, we engage in the debate as to whether we are alone in the world or if there is a connection to spiritual energy that binds us to each other. Our culture teaches us that death is that most solitary act, one that we each must experience alone. But death and loss also provide us with a spontaneous opportunity to explore our spiritual selves and perhaps challenge the limits our culture imposes.

Soul's Pain

Snatched from my throat is the very breath I needed to survive.
Gasping, grasping, for now I must learn to do it on my own.
Ripped from my chest is the heart that only knew how to beat for one.

Like shards of glass tearing through the flesh, tears of blood drip
from the soul that has been torn from this now empty shell.
Never again to feel whole, complete. Drifting in a world of
emptiness, loneliness, sadness.

Hoping one day to fill the empty shell once again with a love unknown
to many-hoping to fill it once again with you.
—Theresa Venero

Hypnagogia: Between Waking and Sleeping

When it is dark enough, you can see the stars.

—Charles Beard

How do you feel late at night, when it's very quiet? What do you think about before you go to sleep? When you are able to lay down your head with a minimum of stress—either because you've started to put your life back in order or you've found a way to give yourself a break—your mind is free to rest. But even more interestingly, your mind is also free to roam. I do some of my best thinking at night, just before I fall asleep. I find that complex problems can become very simple; sometimes answers come to me in mere seconds.

The state of consciousness between wakefulness and sleep is called *hypnagogia*. It is beautifully described in a tenth century Tantric text: "In order to acquire continuity of consciousness, you must hold yourself at the junction of all the states, which constitutes the links between sleeping, dreaming, and waking: the half-sleep or Fourth State." My fascination with this state of mind has been with me for as long as I can remember. Even as a child, when there had been a lot on my mind, it was always a time to ponder, process, and attempt to sort out the complexities of all that troubled me.

At other times when there were no problems at all, I was able to stay in this semiconscious state for an hour. Streams of thoughts and feelings would come and go, like the ebb and flow of the ocean. At such times as these, there is no rhyme or reason for what happens;

41

I am just a passive receiver of my internal universe.

I have vivid recollections of this phenomenon as early as three or four years of age. I specifically recall colorful waves of random faces, places, and unintelligible symbols that appeared to float past my head in the darkness. I recall bringing these objects to my mother's attention, since at the time she was also attempting to get some sleep nearby.

"Mom, what are those *things* floating up in the air?"

"What are you talking about?" she responded, half-asleep.

"Those things floating up there past my head," I persisted.

"Where?" she replied in the dark, moonlit room.

"There," I said, pointing my index finger up into the sky.

Mom looked up, paused, and said, "Oh, it's just your imagination! Go to sleep already. It's way past your bedtime."

So that's how I learned not to ask any more of *those* questions. I just continued to lie back and enjoy the show.

This dreamlike phenomenon has always been part of my pre-sleep experience. If I wanted to I could choose to pay close attention to it, which immediately made the images more vivid and animated. I would vigilantly look around in the darkness to find some sense in the phenomenon, which was generally fruitless. Or more often, I found the experience to be something that would keep my mind busy and my body from getting proper rest. So over the years, I tended to ignore the whole dreamlike state of mind so that I would awaken in the morning with enough hours of sleep to start the day.

Many, many, years later, by the time I entered my forties, I had gotten into the habit of asking myself and others about all kinds of psychic phenomena: soul mates, spirit guides, angels, *everything*. My curiosity and inherent willingness to explore a multitude of possible truths sent me on a journey to learn as much as I could about these fascinating concepts. I began reading everything I could put my hands on regarding these subjects and attended many professional conferences.

In August 2000, I had an opportunity to see Dr. Raymond Moody lecture in person. He spoke freely about his own personal evolution and was not afraid to talk about soul consciousness after death. I was impressed. So I figured, "Who better to ask about my life-long ability to have an altered state of consciousness before sleep?" I decided to be brave and approached Dr. Moody right after his lecture.

Searching for the right words, I asked Dr. Moody, "Have you ever heard of seeing objects or symbols in the dark just before going to sleep? I used to have this experience a lot as a child." Then I paused and waited for him to look at me like I had two heads.

Dr. Moody smiled and without hesitation, replied, "Sure! It's called hypnagogia."

"If you get a book by Andreas Mavromatis, you can read all about it." This was the first time I had ever heard the term and boy, was I excited! Not only did I find out that I wasn't having crazy hallucinations, but I learned someone had actually found the phenomenon common enough to write a book about it.

I quickly purchased the book Dr. Moody recommended, and I was pleasantly surprised to discover that Mavromatis, a British university professor and researcher, was even more interested in hypnagogic phenomena than I was. He spent years investigating its multiple connections to all other "altered states of consciousness," including meditation, hypnosis, REM sleep (dreams) and the general potential of man's creative mind.

Mavromatis discovered that studies of the phenomenon have existed in modern literature as far back as 1848. However, actual reference to hypnagogic experiences extends as far back as Aristotle, who remarked that anyone can convince himself of their occurrence "if he attends to and tries to remember the affections we experience when sinking into slumber, and in the moment of awakening, surprise the images which present themselves to him in sleep."[1]

Soon, after doing more Internet research, I found that even

Thomas Edison had used hypnagogia as a way to assist himself in thinking creatively:

"Edison used to work very hard in his research—at beta, the faster brain wave frequencies. Then when he would reach a 'sticking point' he would take one of his 'cat naps.' He would doze off in his favourite chair, holding steel balls in the palms of his hands. As he would fall asleep—drifting into alpha—his arms would relax and lower, letting the balls fall into pans on the floor. The noise would wake Edison and very often he would awaken with an idea to continue with his project."[2]

This newfound understanding of hypnagogia made it even clearer to me that *all* states of consciousness (described as both "normal" and "altered") are within the realm of one's normal and often spontaneous experience. This awareness is connected to some of my earliest childhood memories and helped in setting the stage for my future life's interest and work.

✦ Chapter 8 ✦

While We Sleep:
Embracing Universal Consciousness

Consciousness is the basis of all life and the field of all possibilities.
Its nature is to expand and unfold its full potential.
The impulse to evolve is thus inherent in the very nature of life.

—Maharishi Mahesh Yogi

The mind is able to tap into much, much, more when external stimuli are not interfering with thought, as often occurs spontaneously just before sleep or upon awakening. The phenomenon of hypnagogia is just one example of this extrasensory inquiry. This seeking of greater knowledge takes many forms. Carl Jung, an early twentieth-century Swiss psychiatrist, was one of the founders of analytical psychology. His unique and unconventional approach to psychology attempted to combine the worlds of philosophy, dreams, mythology, and religion. In traditional psychological terms, Jung would have referred to this wealth of knowledge as the mind being able to access the universal consciousness. However, in Jung's time, mixing spiritual inquiry and problems of the earth plane was not considered within the realm of scientific study.

As noted earlier, Thomas Edison used a pre-sleep, dreamlike state of mind to tap into the mind's creative energies. But my experience has shown me that insights may be discovered *during* sleep itself. Sleep and dream states represent daily, natural opportunities to access the wisdom of the universal consciousness, higher self, the Divine, or however else you choose to describe the process. Haven't you had the experience of going to sleep with a

45

big problem on your mind, only to find out hours later that you have awakened to a great solution? Haven't you caught yourself trying to give someone advice on an issue, telling that person they may have to "sleep on it" first? Doesn't it *always* seem a little clearer the next day?

There is a natural way to program your mind to access such wisdom during sleep. Here is a simple process that I have found works well:

1. Name or clearly describe your problem in your head or say it out loud.
2. Consciously acknowledge the fact that you are responsible and a co-creator of solutions for your problem. Since we are born with the ability to make free choices, we have to decide whether to seek help or work alone. If you believe as I do, that you have spirit guides, guardian angels, or God waiting to help you on the other side, just *ask* for their help.
3. Clearly state your intention, silently or out loud, to resolve the problem.
4. Lastly, affirm that the spiritual universe, via the Law of Attraction, will assist you by the time morning arrives.

Some of the pages of this book were created in exactly the same way. Sometimes I couldn't wait for help until the morning, so I left a pad of paper and pen by my bed in case I woke up in the middle of the night with pages of information in my head that needed to be recorded before they dissipated back to lost consciousness.

There also exists the art of consciously directed dreaming, otherwise known as lucid dreaming. The term, coined by Frederik van Eeden, refers to the "lucid" realization that one is dreaming in the midst of the dream. Often this realization is triggered by the dreamer noticing something impossible or unlikely in the dream, such as flying or meeting the deceased. Once the dreamer has become lucid, he or she may then exert a degree of control over the content of the dream, or "direct" the dream's action to achieve a desired outcome, or arrive at the solution to a particular problem. Sometimes the limitations we impose on ourselves inhibit our ability to clearly see a situation; its causes and remedies. Like the other altered states of consciousness we have discussed, lucid dreaming provides yet another opportunity to more freely search our souls for answers.

Chapter 9

Hypnosis: A Path to Past Lives

What you bring forth out of yourself from the inside will save you. What you do not bring forth out of yourself from the inside will destroy you.

—Gospel of Thomas, first century A.D.

The conscious mind that operates during our day-to-day living is a mind that is very, very, busy. Thousands of random thoughts come and go during the day and there is an ongoing struggle to filter out unneeded information so that one can focus on the task at hand. External stimuli in the form of radio, television, crowds, or any form of visual distraction or auditory interference make it very difficult to pay attention to any one thing. Overall, the conscious mind's ability to concentrate is only at the rate of about twenty-five percent.[1]

In the background of the mind is a consciousness that is very observant and collects data from all levels of experience on an ongoing basis each day. The subconscious mind collects a wealth of information, but it usually doesn't come to the forefront of one's consciousness until life's busy-ness is put at bay. This state of consciousness, as noted earlier, occurs naturally just before sleep or soon after awakening, while spontaneously daydreaming, or upon entering any type of meditative state. Earlier, we reviewed how being in this state of mind is both relaxing and gives access to one's creative energies. In addition, the subconscious mind is also the repository of all memory; the ability to focus and concentrate rises above the ninety-five percent rate.[2]

The easiest way to access subconscious memory is through a

natural phenomenon called hypnosis. Like meditation, hypnosis is an altered state of consciousness that is very relaxing and peaceful. It is also often experienced spontaneously: How often have you traveled to work in a light trance, realizing afterward that you had no idea how you suddenly arrived at your destination? Or how often have you stared at a television set without any awareness about what show is on? Another good example takes place in a movie theater: How often has your consciousness been completely captivated by the characters or events in a movie? All three of these examples represent experiences of being in light hypnotic trance states.

Hypnosis works best with the guidance of a coach or trained therapist. However, the altered state of consciousness cannot be attempted unless the person being hypnotized is ready and able to do the actual work, which requires sustained focus and imagination. Therefore, this means that all hypnosis is actually *self*-hypnosis.

The ability to experience a hypnotic, trance-like state has been known to exist throughout recorded history and even earlier. Ancient Egyptian and Greek records describe hypnotically induced accounts of what were called dream-incubation centers.[3] In fact, many experts point to Adam's experience in the Garden of Eden as the earliest written account of hypnosis. "And the Lord God caused a deep sleep to fall upon Adam, and he slept; and He took one of his ribs, and closed up the flesh instead thereof; And the rib, which the Lord God had taken from man, made He a woman" (Genesis 2:21-22).

In modern times, hypnosis became a reliable way to suggest to a patient that he or she need not experience pain during medical procedures, even during surgery. From 1845 to 1850, James Esdaile (1809-1859), a Scottish surgeon, performed over 300 painless major surgeries without the need of anesthesia. Nineteen of these surgeries were amputations!

However, before hypnosis as an anesthetic gained worldwide acceptance, it was discovered that if certain chemicals could be administered to patients, the patients could be numbed more quickly and easily. Nitrous oxide, ether, and chloroform were found to be quite effective (though the risk of overdose and other side effects was more significant). The surgeon needed no special training—unlike if he were to use hypnosis—and the amount of time spent in relaxing the patient was much shorter when administering chemicals. Also, virtually all patients responded to chemical administration whereas not all patients were hypnotizable. Therefore, the use of chemical medications gained worldwide acceptance and the use of hypnosis for medical purposes became obsolete.

It wouldn't be until the mid 1900s when hypnosis would gain widespread acceptance in clinical practice. However, its popularity was no longer affiliated with physical ailments or helping the mind to cope with medical maladies. Instead, it was found that hypnosis could help the mind cope with addiction and overall emotional problems. Both the American Medical Association and the American Psychological Association formally recognized the vast potential benefits of hypnosis as an adjunct to traditional psychotherapy in 1958.[4]

For example, when a client is troubled by serious emotional problems but he or she is unable to figure out how or when the problem originated, hypnosis has been a very useful technique in helping to identify the source of the problem, usually by recovering lost memories which formed in childhood. These lost memories can include dealing with issues like abandonment and/or abuse.

For the general public not involved in therapy, hypnosis may be most associated with the coaching of individuals to help them stop smoking or lose weight: Many studies have shown its effectiveness in smoking cessation, and weight-loss programs have also proven to be highly successful.[5]

The general public also has a fear of hypnosis due to the widespread exposure to what is called stage hypnosis.

"Will I be made to do something silly, like barking like a dog?" some of my clients ask.

"No, not at all!" I assure them. "You always maintain complete control over your behavior."

The truth is that those volunteers drawn from a large group are generally the most open to *anyone's* suggestion, whether within a trance state or just in simple social conversation. In addition, in a large social gathering, some of these same people *want* to perform for their peer group (or at least enjoy a lot of attention), either consciously or subconsciously. Therefore, stage hypnosis is known to professional practitioners as an atypical form of hypnosis in which participants—both hypnotists and subjects—actually collude to perform publicly.

Clinical hypnosis, which takes place in a private office setting, is a process that requires the client's active interest and participation. The psychotherapist is only an expert coach and the client retains complete control throughout the trance experience. While the therapist gently guides the client through a series of steps designed to induce the hypnotic trance, it is the client who ultimately permits the trance to occur.

In order to clarify this dual mental process, let's return to the analogy of being fully entranced or engaged in a great movie or favorite book. Your attention and emotions are fully involved in the setting, the characters, and the mood of each moment. But at the same time, another part of your brain is cognizant that you are not in the movie or book. If you have any conflict or discomfort, you know you can just turn your head away and disengage from the experience.

The choice is the same while one is fully absorbed in the reexperiencing of a deep memory. The subject can choose to either pursue the unfolding adventure at hand, communicate the desire to move away from the experience, or simply open his or her eyes. The subject always retains this prerogative. So it may relieve you to know that the choice to involve a professional to help you retrieve deep-seated or even past life memories is one that can be made without apprehension or fear.

What are the chances you can retrieve past life memories if you are highly motivated and you have enlisted the help of a good professional? The answer varies widely from one individual to another. Most people are capable of reaching the depth of trance necessary, but a small percentage, even if they are willing, are not able to be hypnotized easily. This can be properly assessed by a trained professional. Considering all such factors, most practitioners have found that when working with a motivated subject, approximately four out of ten subjects are able to recover at least some aspects of past life memory on the first try.

Does acceptance of what appears to be a past life memory require a belief in the notions of karma or reincarnation? Does entertaining the idea that you may have lived before need to conflict with your religious affiliation or identity? These are questions we have all wondered about at one time or another. In the next chapter, I'll share my personal journey with you and we can explore some of these questions together.

Chapter 10

Is Reincarnation Real?

It is not more surprising to be born twice than once;
everything in nature is resurrection.

—Voltaire

When a client is helped, under hypnosis, to recover memories from a time before birth, the individual often reports firsthand visual images, sounds, and bodily sensations associated with events that seem like actual memories of a past life. Could some of this be a product of something the client read or saw on television? Or perhaps some people have a very vivid imagination. It is possible that the memories may come from a variety of experiences, but in clinical practice it is important to believe that all the information that comes from the mind is important and has profound meaning.

After a regression session is completed, the experience is analyzed in depth. The client whose experience is vague or whose images seem to represent more of a collage of experiences is often unsure whether to consider it actual memory or something else. Again, it may not matter whether the experience actually took place historically, because it invariably has profound relevance and important psychological meaning to the client.

So, is there really such a thing as a past life experience? Couldn't it be that in a trance state you can actually channel others' experiences? Or is it possible to access a field of knowledge Carl Jung called the "collective" or "universal consciousness?" Nevertheless, most of the world believes in reincarnation. A significant percentage of the American public also believes that a soul may travel from lifetime to lifetime. According to various Gallup polls over the years, about twenty-eight to forty percent of the American public believes in reincarnation.

In my personal research, I have found *thousands* of books and extensive articles written about the subject. Throughout recorded history, the issue of reincarnation has been addressed by many philosophers, writers, and leaders since ancient times, including the Early Christian Gnostics.

In modern times, the issue of reincarnation continues to be a source of curiosity and interest for most Americans. In the past, most Westerners were exposed to the idea through their knowledge of ancient Hindu or Buddhist traditions. However, a resurgence of interest has arisen via the renewed interest in The Holy Kabbalah, the mystical tradition affiliated with Judaism. The three greatest books of Kabbalism are the Sefer Yetzirah: The Book of Formation; the Sefer ha Zohar: The Book of Splendor; and the Apocalypse: The Book of Revelation. The following is a quote from the Sefer ha Zohar:

> "The souls must re-enter the Absolute, from whence they have emerged. But to accomplish this end they must develop the perfections; the germ of which is planted in them. And if they have not developed these traits in this one life, then they must commence another, a third, and so forth. They must go on like this until they acquire the condition that allows them to associate again with God."[1]

Currently, the sources of information on the subject seem almost limitless. A sample Google search on the subject returned over 700,000 hits, or sources of information. My personal interest in reincarnation began when I was formally introduced to the calming practice of Transcendental Meditation at the tender age of nineteen. Since being exposed to this simple notion of peace and harmony,

Eastern traditions of life and spirit have fascinated me.

I have always wondered about everyone's spiritual or religious beliefs, no doubt due to my own family history and personal upbringing. My mother, Mary Kathryn Sullivan, was of Irish descent and raised in the Presbyterian faith. Her first husband, William Harrell, was Welsh and introduced her to the Mormon religion. When Bill died, she met my father, Irving Scheinberg, who was Jewish and of Austrian and Polish descent. Since my father did not have a strong allegiance to his religion or his family in general, my mother was free to raise us five children in the Mormon faith.

I grew up in the 60s, at the height of the Vietnam War. The atrocities of "containing communism" were shown every evening after dinner on the six o'clock news. There was no government censorship on war coverage like there is today. I saw women and children burned with napalm bombs. Then, every night's newscast ended with an honor roll call of countless war casualties, most of whom were only a few years older than I was.

In horror and disbelief, I was bold enough to ask my local church leaders if our religion took a firm stand against such insanity. After all, didn't God say, "Thou Shalt Not Kill?" To my great disappointment, I was told that the policy of the church was not to contest government decisions regarding war.

Soon, I came to discover that the only religious organization that took a firm stance against the war, or *any* war for that matter, was the Quakers. So I was left with the impression that maybe a minority religion may have had some better ideas than what most commonly believed in my community.

As if it wasn't confusing enough being an Irish Mormon with a Jewish last name, my parents raised me in a predominantly Italian Catholic neighborhood. There I met and later married my wife, Geraldine, who was raised Italian Catholic. By the time our son Jared was born, I decided to defer his religious affiliation to my wife's Catholic orientation.

Throughout my life, I gained an appreciation of *all* major

religious traditions: Christian, Judaic, Western, and Eastern. It became important to understand not so much the differences between religions, but more often the spiritual commonalities among them all. Ultimately, all religious organizations emphasize the importance of being compassionate and of service to others and God, as well as following some version of the Golden Rule: treat others as you wish to be treated.

So what about the issue of reincarnation? Western religions tend to profess the notion that we have only one life on this earth. Eastern religions tend to teach that the soul not only transcends one's lifetime, but that it lives on through many physical incarnations. Furthermore, Eastern religion teaches that the soul evolves continuously throughout each lifetime, since each life experience prompts the attainment of profound karmic lessons.

I do not consider myself an expert on *any* religion, even Mormonism, the one Christian religion that I studied every week in Sunday school. So I have done much research to get a general idea of what great scholars have debated over the past few centuries regarding the concept of reincarnation. The most provocative quest debated by those who have spent a lifetime studying theology is this: "If there is such a thing as reincarnation, why isn't it mentioned in the Bible?" The answer is complex. First of all, many scholars report that there are *many* references to reincarnation in the Bible. For example, in John 9:2, the disciples asked Jesus, "Rabbi, who sinned, this man or his parents, that he was born blind?" If *paying for one's sin* means having to be born blind, then scholars believe the implication is that the man had to pay some kind of karmic debt for a transgression he committed in a previous lifetime.

In Matthew 17:12-13, Jesus said, "Elijah has already come, and they did not know him, but did to him whatever they pleased. So also the son of man will suffer at their hands. Then the disciples understood that he was speaking to them of John the Baptist."

In Matthew 11:11-15, Jesus said, "Truly, I say to you, among those born of women there has risen no one greater than John the

Baptist...and if you are willing to accept it, he is Elijah who is to come. He who has ears to hear, let him hear."

Other scholars state that most biblical references to reincarnation were censored when Roman Emperor Constantine the Great called the Second Council of Constantinople in A.D. 553. The council consisted of dozens of the most powerful political leaders of that time period. The task was to determine which of the original writings or canons available should be included in the final official version of the Bible. There are dozens of ancient scriptures, as well as other sacred writings, that never made it into the final edited versions of what is called the Bible.[2]

Once the powerful council reached its decision, Constantine decreed that the final version of the Bible would be the *only* version of the Bible available. The populace was told to adopt the agreed-upon edition and destroy all other versions. The stakes were high: Anyone who was found to possess any other version of the sacred scriptures faced charges of heresy. The punishment for heresy was quite harsh: "perpetrators" faced long terms of imprisonment or even death, although Constantine later realized that some heretics actually welcomed "martyrdom," so such harsh punishments actually did not work.[3]

Could it be that those powerful leaders may have been concerned about canonical references to reincarnation? Could warnings of mortal punishment and death have become less threatening to peasants who realized that not only would their souls survive death, but would be able to incarnate in a whole other body a short time later?

As a young Mormon who grew up on Long Island, I learned in Sunday school that my church organization didn't form until 1830. The Church of Jesus Christ of Latter-day Saints (another name for the Mormon religion) originated with a young man, Joseph Smith, who was confused by the differences in the world's religions. So he embarked on his own personal quest for divine guidance and inspiration. After many months of turmoil and prayer, he was able to find (according to the teachings of the Mormon faith) actual proof of Jesus Christ's presence during ancient times in the New World, in a geographical location that would be later known as New York. The complete story would be later described in a new sacred text known as the Book of Mormon.

Since I grew up in a predominantly Italian Catholic neighborhood (and I was the only Mormon in my school), none of my friends had even heard about the book my family regarded as the most sacred. But nonetheless, my mother told me that the Book of Mormon was a "second witness" to the Divine's presence in the Western world, and that's what made Latter Day Saints special. Furthermore, Mormons believe that the Holy Scriptures, their version of the Bible as translated by Joseph Smith, was the most accurate version. Yet all my Catholic friends told me that their priests believed only the New American Bible, which adapted the King James Version to the modern American language in 1970.

As I got older, I wondered more and more how each word of Scripture could be so important, yet the words themselves could be very different from one version to another. In fact, there are at least *five* different popular versions of the Bible: the King James Version, the Holy Scriptures (Joseph Smith translation), the New International Version, the New American Standard, and the New World Translation of the Holy Scriptures (Jehovah's Witnesses).

Since I have no personal training or expertise in such areas, I embarked on an extensive search of formally recognized experts on the Bible. After reviewing hundreds of essays and books from hundreds of ministers and professors of religious studies, I would like to share the viewpoints of a few of those whose work is likely to provoke further interest and soulful reflection.

One such expert is Bart D. Ehrman, an award-winning professor and prolific writer. He is an internationally recognized speaker and scholar and the author or editor of over twenty books, many of which were *New York Times* bestsellers. Dr. Ehrman has wonderful credentials, but beyond this fact, I found myself compelled to read several of his books because I could relate to his upbringing and search for spiritual clarification.

Dr. Ehrman became an Evangelical Christian as a teen. He then proceeded to study the Bible in undergraduate as well as graduate school, eventually receiving his PhD and MDiv from Princeton Theological Seminary. He has since dedicated his lifetime to the exhaustive research of ancient documents.

Ehrman's scholarly research and his personal passion to get to the deeper meaning of his own spiritual beliefs led him to learn the ancient Bible languages for himself.

"I came to see early on that the full meaning and nuance of the Greek text of the New Testament could be grasped only when it is read and studied in the original language; the same thing applies to the Old Testament, as I later learned when I acquired Hebrew."[4]

Dr. Ehrman went on to say that the "original" scripture was written one, two, or even three generations after Christ's death. The Greeks then undertook a massive effort to translate the scripture. Thereafter, almost all the "original" documentation was lost or purposely destroyed.[5] Though we have very few remnants of the original scriptures (among them, possibly those that were found in 1947, known as the Dead Sea Scrolls, and the sacred texts discovered in 1945 at Nag Hammadi), at least 5,000 Greek translations have been discovered. Among the existing Greek copies, at least 30,000 textual variations—ranging from unimportant to quite significant— have been noted by scholars.[6]

Our current English versions are based on different Greek translations that were discovered over the past few centuries. The King James Version was one of the first comprehensive efforts, being compiled as early as 1611. It's no wonder why it has traditionally been the most popular version. However, many other Greek manuscripts have been discovered since that time, and it is now believed by some scholars that the King James translation was actually based on one of the less accurate Greek translations of the original Aramaic writings.[7]

To make matters even more complicated to those of us—myself included—who are not Biblical scholars, identical English translations of the Bible are interpreted differently by a multitude of Bible-based Christian religions. There are literally thousands of Christian religions that quote no more than five versions of the same Bible as the core of their own unique organizational structure, rules, and belief system.

So what did *I* do with all this information? I decided that they *all* make sense. As previously mentioned, I don't care so much about the differences between each religious sect; I'm more interested in the similarities. All religions, including those that are non-Christian, have most of the same core beliefs and values, particularly in regard to reverence for life, and a great respect for a higher power or God that is incomprehensibly greater than us all.

I also believe that Jesus Christ (a Jew) wasn't born to start an array of new religious orders. I believe Christ was here to show all of us how we might live in this confusing and too often violent world. He was here to serve as an example of what we should all strive for in our lifetimes. A supreme example of unwavering and unconditional love, Christ was loving and completely nonjudgmental of everyone, both in word and deed. He was even completely compassionate to those who hurt and whipped him. Rather than judge or punish, he offered service and understanding. Rather than retort and take revenge, he consistently preached peace and complete forgiveness of everyone's ignorance and abusiveness, even as he died on the cross: "Father, forgive them, for they don't know what they are doing" (Luke 23:34). I believe that this is truly what is meant by the intention of following Christ Consciousness.

Did Christ ever clarify the question of whether the soul is able to return to the earthly plane in another body? Aside from the few references noted in the beginning of this chapter, the Bible does not state that to be the case.

Does that mean that the majority of the people in the world who are non-Christians and believe in reincarnation are wrong? No.

All I suggest is that you should not be so quick to pass judgment. Spiritual beliefs are very personal and very sacred. For this reason, I recommend keeping an open mind. Be open to all beliefs, find out which ones resonate with you on the deepest levels, and allow others to do the same for themselves. Respect and love others on their own souls' journey in this life.

I tell clients that it doesn't matter what their belief system states about the issue of reincarnation: "You can enjoy the experience, call it whatever you want, and you may still be deeply moved."

Finding myself to exist in this world, I believe I shall in some shape or other always exist; and, with all the inconveniences human life is liable to, I shall not object to a new edition of mine, hoping, however, that the 'errata' of the last may be corrected.
—Benjamin Franklin
(author, politician, scientist, inventor, statesman; 1706-1790)

Before I decided to involve myself in formal training in past life regression therapy, like some of my clients, I didn't know *what* to believe. At first, the concept of reincarnation sounded as far-fetched idea to me as it may seem to you as you are reading this chapter. But I found the possibility of past lives fascinating. I'm the kind of guy who loves hovering over the earth gazing at trees and meadows in a hot air balloon. So why not be adventurous and explore my inner landscape?

While in my second day of training, which was to include a personal attempt of recalling a past life experience, I decided to put all fears aside and trust the recovery process. I was, in turn, rewarded with what appeared to be such a vivid, moving, firsthand experience that I instantly became a believer.

The best way to describe it is to liken it to a hauntingly familiar song, a conversation with a family member, or even a topic on *Oprah* that instantly triggers a very old childhood memory. A sound, smell, or environment suddenly brings to mind something you hadn't thought about for a long, long time. The image and associated feelings become so powerful that you just know the memory to be true. When you have had that kind of experience, no one can convince you otherwise. In this way, almost all of my clients who recover vivid memories, regardless of their previous religious orientation, become believers as well. Usually they do not find that it conflicts with or challenges their religious beliefs. In fact, it almost always enhances any spiritual foundation to which they already subscribe. St. Teresa of Avila described this most intimate level of being as one's "Interior Castle". Such a deep journey cannot help but gratify anyone doing soul-searching on their own.

> *Read me, O Reader, if you find delight in me, because very*
> *seldom shall I come back into this world.*
> —Leonardo da Vinci
> (mathematician, sculptor, painter, inventor, musician,
> engineer; 1452-1519)

Lastly, in seeking the answer to whether reincarnation is real or not, one must look into the availability of actual scientific research on the subject. Through my exploration of data on the subject, I have found countless anecdotal records of individuals who were regressed to a previous lifetime and then later able to find historical proof that such a lifetime did indeed exist.

As a child, I remember my mother telling me about a Colorado woman named Virginia Tighe. Under hypnosis in 1952, she reported that in 1806 she was an eight-year-old girl living in Cork, Ireland. "Bridey Murphy" spoke in detail about her mother, father, and her future husband, named Sean Brian McCarthy.

As the hypnotist Morey Bernstein wrote in his best-selling book, *The Search for Bridey Murphy*, Tighe gave so much detail regarding people and places during her regression session that Bernstein was later able to verify much of her account through actual historical records.

Many years later, I read about the devout Christian, medically intuitive psychic Edgar Cayce (1877-1945). Cayce left a legacy of over 1,400 transcripts of channeled psychic readings, many of which mentioned past life information. However, most of the information Cayce reported was not historically verifiable. Since much of the data referred back to ancient times, specific records to prove his facts were not available. Yet Cayce's proven track record for medical diagnosis and treatment—as well as his amazing prophetic abilities—have given the Association for Research and Enlightenment, a group formed to study Cayce's body of work, plenty of scientific data to study for years to come.

Most recently, a 2007 video documentary called *Past Life Investigation* produced by the Canadian Broadcasting Corporation was highlighted on *Oprah* (televised on June 24, 2008). The video highlighted the actual past life regression session of a Canadian woman named Natasha. This twenty-nine-year-old Roman Catholic didn't believe in reincarnation, but in trance (under hypnosis) she recalled a life in 1930 as a peasant woman traveling from Nepal to India to sell her goods. She was able to speak some Hindi words and names, even though she had no previous exposure to the culture. The border town in India she called "Anji" did not even appear on geographical maps. But when Sarah Kapoor, the reporter and host of the documentary, found the village on a fifty-year-old map, she and Natasha were able to fly to the area and verify all the previously reported information as quite plausible.

There are many reports of people who are drawn to certain locations as tourists, only to discover later that they seem to already be quite familiar with the area they are visiting. They report feeling a sense of déjà vu, a sensation that they have been there before. Could this be a fact or just a feeling? In some cases, a tourist has been able to describe the history of an object or place more accurately than the tour guide who is supposedly introducing it to his group.

There are thousands of other well-documented anecdotes that strongly evidence reincarnation—but skeptics are prone to react to such stories with the explanation that these individuals may have heard about such places before, or that they may have read about the history of the location at an earlier time in their lives. Such individuals may report that they have recovered memories from a previous lifetime, but skeptics might say that they actually recovered memories from a previous conversation or a long-forgotten history lesson. Ultimately, the benefits of the past life regression experience and the insights that it provides are not dependent on a solid belief in reincarnation, though such an experience usually convinces even the most ardent skeptic.

ᴄⱷᴄ **Chapter 11** ᴄⱷᴄ

Children Who Remember Past Lives

It is again a strong proof of men knowing most things before birth,
that when mere children they grasp innumerable facts with such
speed as to show that they are not then taking them in
for the first time, but remembering or recalling them.

—Cicero (Roman statesman, lawyer, philosopher; 106-43 B.C.)

I have found that the most convincing scientific proof of reincarnation comes from studies that do not involve adults at all. These studies don't involve hypnosis, either. Instead, they emanate from children as young as two years of age. Coming from the mouths of babes, these children talk spontaneously about people and events that are often initially believed by their parents to be imaginary. In many cases, the children insist that the stories are real and that they happened when they "were big." Many of these children have been able to describe vivid details of their past lives including their names, their hometowns, their occupations, and even the manner in which they died! There are literally *thousands* of documented accounts of young children who speak about memories of previous lifetimes.

Here in the United States, author and reincarnationist Joan Grant (1907-1989) was one of the first to document memories of the past lives she recalled as a young child. Her highly acclaimed first work, *Winged Pharaoh* (1937) was an insightful historical novel which launched her literary career. She later acknowledged that *Winged Pharaoh* was actually written while she was in a trance-like state, recalling the lifetime she believed herself to have lived. Joan published a total of fifteen novels and revealed that her memories of at least seven distinct past lives formed the basis for much of her work. Her vivid memories of three separate lives as an Egyptian had such clarity and detail that she was able to read Egyptian hieroglyphics.

> *As far back as I can remember I have unconsciously referred to the experiences of a previous state of existence.*
> —Henry David Thoreau (American author; 1817-1862)

Children who remember languages from previous lives are indeed rare, but I have come across a few well-documented cases in my research. Dr. Adrian Finkelstein wrote about several such cases in his book, *Your Past Lives and the Healing Process (1996)*. Most notable was the case of a five-year-old boy from Los Angeles, California, who often spoke in a language that his mother could not understand. Investigation revealed that the boy was actually speaking an obscure dialect from Northern Tibet. There was nothing in the child's current life experience or environment to account for this remarkable linguistic ability.[1]

Dr. Ian Stevenson (1918-2007) was a pioneer who researched reports of children's past lives for over forty years.[2] As a medical doctor and former head of the Department of Psychiatry at the University of Virginia, Dr. Stevenson traveled all around the world and compiled over 2,500 case studies based on children's past lives. The wealth of information he was able to gather enabled him to scientifically investigate, corroborate, and validate a significant percentage of these cases.

Another such investigator, Jim B. Tucker, left his private practice in psychiatry in 1996 to pursue his own research into the phenomenon. Dr. Tucker, now a child psychiatrist at the University of Virginia, extensively reviewed many of Dr. Stevenson's case studies. With the spirit of a good detective, his theories, explanations, and revelations are detailed in his book, *Life Before Life (2008)*.

Tucker relates a particularly fascinating story of a child who reported having a previous life as his grandfather. Sam Taylor never knew his paternal grandfather, having been born a year and a half after the elder man's death. At the age of eighteen months, while his father was changing his diaper, Sam remarked, "When I was your age, I used to change *your* diapers." Initially, Sam's father didn't take the odd comment seriously, until other evidence began to surface. In time, Sam demonstrated uncanny knowledge of many specific details of his grandfather's life that he would have no other way of knowing. [3]

Forget not that I shall come back to you… A little while, a moment of rest upon the wind, and another woman shall bear me.

—Kahlil Gibran

(Lebanese-American artist, poet, philosopher and theologian 1883-1931)

Trutz Hardo, a popular European author, lecturer, and regression therapist, is one of many researchers who believe that bodily markings may be an indication of "cellular memory" that is passed from one lifetime to the next. He has found that these markings may corroborate a verbal description of a violent end in a previous life. In his book, *Children Who Have Lived Before(1988)*, Hardo tells an amazing story about a three-year-old boy who was born with a long red birthmark which stretched across the top of his head. The boy was able to give very specific details of his past life identity, including the community in which he had lived as well as his violent death. His vivid description led investigators to the gruesome discovery of his previous body and the confession of his former neighbor, who had split his skull with an axe![4]

It is not surprising that many of these cases originated in countries where cultural and religious beliefs accept and even embrace the concept of reincarnation. Parents, teachers, and medical professionals in these regions of the world are far more open to the idea that their children's amazing stories may be based in fact. After all, it is well known and widely accepted that the Dalai Lama was positively identified at the age of two as the reincarnation of the

Thirteenth Dalai Lama who died in 1933. Elders were thoroughly convinced of his identity when he was able to identify his disguised "visitors" by their proper names and able to recall specific details of his past life as the Thirteenth Dalai Lama. This two-year-old even spoke the same dialect of Central Tibet, which was an unknown dialect in the district of his birth. In western cultures, on the other hand, parents may be quick to dismiss their children's memories as just a product of a vivid imagination.

Not all parents do this, however. Carol Bowman from Pennsylvania was faced with a puzzling situation. Her five-year-old son, Chase, had an unusually negative reaction to the loud noises of a July fourth celebration. Concerned by her son's seemingly extreme response, she questioned him about it. To her amazement, Chase began to describe how the noises reminded him of when he was a terrified adult soldier in the midst of a battle! His voice sounded so serious and mature, his description was so detailed, and his body was so tense that she was soon convinced that it all must be true. Other revelations that followed were so amazing that Bowman decided to assemble them together in book form. The result was her first publication, *Children's Past Lives: How Past Life Memories Affect Your Child (1998)*. After several more years of research and information gathering, Bowman published her second book, *Return From Heaven (2003)*. She has chosen to dedicate her entire adult career to helping parents understand how past life memories may affect their children, and has created an excellent Web site for further information on this fascinating subject: www.childpastlives.org.

So, if your child spontaneously and matter-of-factly mentions information about his "other mommy" or "other family," talks about a personal experience that couldn't possibly have taken place in his lifetime, or has an unusual or irrational fear that can't possibly be explained by his current limited experience, consider the possibility that such occurrences may have nothing to do with your child's imagination. It just may be a matter of residual recollections from earlier experiences that occurred in a prior lifetime. In the very young these memories are unfiltered, unedited, and relatively fresh. They can often emerge as soon as the child develops sufficient language skills to articulate them. As the child grows older, these distinct memories can begin to fade and recede into the subconscious. At this point, the remnants of that previous set of experiences may be reduced to unusual talents or unexplained aptitudes for things they have not (in their current lifetime) been exposed to.

Consider the thousands of documented cases of child prodigies. These young children exhibit inexplicable skills and abilities in music or the arts by the time they are six or seven years old, even while their fine motor skills are still forming. They are able to learn and absorb information at phenomenal speeds and master college level math or science before they are old enough to enter high school. Are these simply magical gifts bestowed upon a little human being at birth, or could it be that some deep memory of skills attained in a previous lifetime has been carried over to the present?

Believing as I do in the theory of rebirth, I live in the hope that if not in this birth, in some other birth I shall be able to hug all humanity in friendly embrace.
—Mohandas Karamchand Gandhi
(Indian political and spiritual leader; 1869–1948)

Now let's consider the evolution of mankind in general. What was learned in a life before must somehow follow us into the next life so that we as individuals, and the human race as a species, are able to grow ever wiser and more enlightened with each new generation. We could not possibly learn the entirety of human knowledge and understanding that represents our current cumulative evolution in a single lifetime. It stands to reason that we as human beings are born with a greater volume of knowledge and ability than our ancestors and that the generations that come after us will have even more. Just as today's human being has grown taller and enjoys greater longevity and greater brain mass than his predecessors, it follows then that his soul has grown and developed as well over the ages. This offers us rather strong evidence of the soul's ability to remember.

Could it be that the souls of all those who incarnated before us retained some of what they learned and carried it forward with them, gradually evolving into the relatively humane and civilized people that have inherited the earth today? I would like to think so. This earthly existence is filled with so many of God's creatures and divine lessons to learn that I can't imagine God would expect that any one of us could possibly appreciate it all in one short lifetime.

Once again, it really doesn't matter whether or not you want to believe in the idea of reincarnation. Feel free to call it an overactive imagination or the mind under hypnosis being able to access other dimensions of time or space. Ultimately, the personal experience of what is called past life regression is always a fascinating and profoundly moving adventure. More importantly, it can be an important adjunct to the deep insight that is sought in more traditional psychotherapy modalities. More than one client has told me that having one two-hour session has given them as much insight as six months of psychotherapy. Others tell me that they can't even compare the process to traditional psychotherapy because "it's just so much *deeper*." It gives each client an unusually memorable and healing experience. Clients often leave the session feeling more peaceful, spiritual, and closer to God than ever before.

Every soul… comes into this world strengthened by the victories
or weakened by the defeats of its previous life.
Its place in this world as a vessel appointed to honor or dishonor
is determined by its previous merits or demerits.
Its work in this world determines its place
in the world which is to follow this.
—Origen (early church father; 185-254 A.D.)

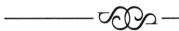
Chapter 12

Case Studies in Past Life Regression

It is the secret of the world that all things subsist and do not die,
but only retire a little from sight and afterwards return again.
Nothing is dead; men feign themselves dead, and endure mock
funerals and mournful obituaries, and there they stand looking out
of the window, sound and well, in some new strange disguise.
—Ralph Waldo Emerson (American essayist, poet, philosopher; 1803-1882)

Hypnosis offers us a vehicle by which we can explore our past life experiences. The key element to successful hypnosis is relaxation. It has been my experience that almost everyone, with some coaching, can achieve a very deep level of relaxation. Most people report the meditation experience at the very beginning of the past life regression session as being "the most relaxed I've ever been my whole life!" It's ironic that this initial phase lasts only about twenty minutes, but it may be one of the few real twenty-minute breaks that a person has given himself during a lifetime filled with busy-ness.

The next phase involves the gentle transition from meditation to hypnosis, followed by an attempt to recover one or two early childhood memories. These memories may have been lost for a very long time, but they are usually reexperienced in amazing detail. The client is encouraged to report their experience using all five senses, so it is easy to accompany them on their journey of rediscovery. As the client's trance deepens, I suggest that their memory is limitless. They may be able to recall events all the way back to birth, as well as experiences in utero. I further suggest that if they wish, they can recall events from a previous lifetime.

I have found that between seventy to eighty percent of my clients have been able to recover what appears to be past life memory during their first try. Much of the statistical variation depends on whether the client has only met me once before (for an introductory session) or if they already know me very well from being one of my traditional psychotherapy clients. Those who know me well naturally feel more comfortable, trusting, and ready for the regression experience, so the success rate is much higher. But even those who are new to the idea are very pleased and gratified after experiencing such a deep level of relaxation. Since the whole regression session usually lasts up to two hours or more, almost *everyone* is happy with whatever tranquility or insight is obtained.

The four stories that follow detail actual transcripts of regression sessions. Each represents a past life regression which yielded an insightful experience and powerful healing. In each case, the client has been in traditional psychotherapy for some time, and has expressed a desire to understand their issues more deeply. Each has also demonstrated an openness to the underlying concepts of spirituality and a willingness to explore the past life regression avenue of inquiry. Each was excited at the possibility of tapping the deepest levels of their being.

You will have the rare opportunity to be a fly on the wall as I coach each client on their own soul-searching adventure, for both past lives and spirit guides. (Since each session lasted over two hours, the transcripts below are abridged versions.) Clients' names have been changed to preserve confidentiality.

Case Study A

Life Should Be Better Than This: Searching For Purpose

Life begins at the end of your comfort zone.

—Neale Donald Walsch

Lauren had been involved in therapy for two years before she met me. She explained that she had been able to address most of her problems with her previous therapist and was in a much better place than when she had first started therapy.

"With my previous therapist, we got to a point where I started to run out of things to talk about. I was able to deal with most of what was bothering me and I felt much better. So a short time later, we mutually decided it was time to finish our sessions," she said.

Then Lauren continued. "I don't know what it is. That was about six months ago and I still have blocks of time when I feel very unhappy, for no particular reason!"

"That must be very frustrating."

"It sure is! And it is starting to drive my husband nuts!"

"What does he say?"

"He says, 'I thought you worked that problem out. What's the matter with you now?'"

"And what do you tell him?"

"I tell him, 'I don't know!' I don't know if it's me or it's him, but he just seems to be getting on my nerves lately." Then she began to cry.

"So you're telling me that you often feel dissatisfied with your husband, but you can't put a finger on *why*?"

"Yeah. Pretty crazy, huh?"

"Not necessarily. Whenever someone has a feeling, there's always a reason behind it; it's just that sometimes it's hard to find the right words to explain a feeling, or explain its origin. But there's always a reason that makes sense. And that's what we can try to figure out together."

"That sounds good. When my friend Debbie told me about her past life regression experience with you, I was fascinated! I thought that if I was going to get back into therapy, this approach might help me get some insight from a whole other angle."

"Well, I hope you get the insight you're looking for. It will certainly be something different from what you've experienced before."

A young woman in her late thirties, Lauren was unhappy and her marriage had begun to reflect the dissatisfaction she and her husband had with one another. She also felt that her life had no purpose or meaning. Despite the considerable progress she had made in her previous therapy, she believed there was more she needed to uncover and resolve. She was enthusiastic and eager to explore whatever this experience had in store for her.

I explained to Lauren that she should plan on having a very deeply relaxing and thought-provoking experience. We would make a sincere attempt to recover early childhood memories. If that was successful, we would continue to seek past life memories. I emphasized that if she was comfortable and ready, there was a good chance she would be able to recover lots of memories.

The following week Lauren arrived ready to begin the regression experience. Soon after she transitioned from meditation to hypnosis, Lauren proceeded to describe a pleasant memory of herself and her father. When she was four, he calmly comforted her after she had experienced a terrible nightmare. It was wonderful to be reassured that her father was always a person with whom she could feel safe. After further prompting, Lauren recovered another wonderful experience. This time, she was only two years old. She described how her mother helped her unwind before going to bed by cradling and rocking her gently in her arms.

Both of these childhood experiences helped remind Lauren that she was indeed loved and that she was treated as special when she was much younger. So far, I did not have a clue as to the source of Lauren's general dissatisfaction with life, or why she felt that her life had no particular purpose or meaning. Once Lauren finished describing her experience as a two-year-old, I proceeded further.

RICH: Let yourself remember. Stay in a very deep relaxed state. Reexperience these memories. I'll give you a few moments to remember this vividly. Do you have a glimpse of anything?

LAUREN: Yes.

RICH: What is that?

LAUREN: I'm in a room. It's old and there's a stone fireplace.

RICH: What else?

LAUREN: A table, like a dining table.

RICH: How does the table look?

LAUREN: It's very thick wood. It looks like it weighs a ton.

RICH: How big is it?

LAUREN: Four or five feet. It's long.

RICH: How many chairs are at the table?

LAUREN: Two. One at each head of the table, and there are benches on either side.

RICH: So there are two chairs at the ends and benches on the sides?

LAUREN: Yes. And it's set for dinner.

RICH: What's for dinner? What do you smell?

[*Lauren's nose wrinkles up.*]

LAUREN: I smell bread and some sort of stew. There is a big black pot in the fireplace.

RICH: It smells good.

LAUREN: Mmmm.

RICH: Who's going to be at the dinner table?

LAUREN: The children.

RICH: How many children?

LAUREN: Five.

RICH: And who else?

LAUREN: There are six; there's a baby. There are seven plates but there is a high chair too.

RICH: Who are you in this family?

LAUREN: The father.

RICH: What do you do next?

[*Lauren doesn't answer. However, I see her eyes darting back and forth under her eyelids.*]

RICH: Well, what happens next?

LAUREN: I'm looking for my wife. She's not in her rocking chair. She's probably with the baby in the back room.

[*I continue to see Lauren's eyes searching.*]

RICH: What happens next?

LAUREN: I go to look for her.

RICH: How are you feeling?

[*Lauren sighs.*]

LAUREN: Tired. I just came home from work.

RICH: What happens next?

LAUREN: I hang up my jacket on the peg by the door. I hear the other kids running around.

RICH: Then what happens?

LAUREN: I hear my wife call to them to wash up for dinner. And I hear the baby crying.

RICH: What happens next?

LAUREN: Um, five children are running to the sink. They see me and they stop.

RICH: And then what?

LAUREN: They say hello and we hug.

RICH: And then what happens?

LAUREN: I tell them to go wash up. I ask my daughter, Sarah;

she's the oldest...

[*Lauren pauses for a while.*]

RICH: How old is she?

LAUREN: Ten.

RICH: Ten.

LAUREN: I ask her where her mother is. She says that she is in the back with James.

RICH: James?

LAUREN: The baby. I pat her on the head and pinch her cheek. Sarah was named after my mother. She looks just like Mary.

RICH: Oh, and Mary is?

LAUREN: My wife.

RICH: Then what happens?

LAUREN: I go to Mary and she is picking up James from his cradle.

RICH: And then what?

LAUREN: She sees me. She smiles and I take James. He's getting big.

RICH: Yeah. And then what happens?

LAUREN: I kiss Mary hello.

RICH: What does she call you?

LAUREN: Thomas.

RICH: Thomas. This is your name?

LAUREN: Yes.

RICH: Okay, Thomas, what happens next?

LAUREN: Mary tells me to wash up for dinner.

RICH: And then what?

LAUREN: I follow her out. All of the other children are sitting at the table. There's Sarah, and there's David.

RICH: How old is David?

LAUREN: Nine. And there's Edward.

RICH: How old is he?

LAUREN: Seven.

RICH: Who else?

LAUREN: Francis.

RICH: Francis. How old (is he)?

LAUREN: Five.

RICH: Francis is a boy?

LAUREN: Yes.

RICH: Okay.

LAUREN: And Elizabeth.

RICH: Elizabeth. Okay, how old is she?

LAUREN: Two. [*Lauren pauses and thinks.*] Actually a little older: two and a half.

RICH: And then there's James.

LAUREN: Yes.

RICH: And your wife, Mary. How old is she?

LAUREN: Thirty.

RICH: How old are you?

LAUREN: Thirty. We grew up together.

RICH: What is your last name?

LAUREN: [*Thinks for a moment.*] MacIntyre.

[*So far, Lauren has presented me with a very clear picture of Thomas and his family. I start to silently wonder where this past life adventure will lead.*]

RICH: Okay, so here you are all ready for dinner. What happens next?

LAUREN: Mary puts James in the high chair, which is next to her. Sarah is next to Elizabeth. She already started serving. She helps her mother a lot.

RICH: Your older daughter, Sarah, is very nice.

LAUREN: Yes. She has bread wrapped in a towel on the table and she put the stew in everybody's bowls. She is helping Elizabeth.

RICH: Sarah is a very good daughter.

LAUREN: Yes.

RICH: Who does she look like?

LAUREN: Mary. Exactly like Mary.

RICH: What does Mary look like?

LAUREN: She has a darkish blonde hair. Very tiny. She has soft blue eyes.

RICH: What is she wearing?

LAUREN: An off-white blouse and she has a jumper (with) some shade of brown over it. And an apron. She has her hair pulled back and she looks tired.

RICH: Okay. What happens next?

LAUREN: David says the blessing; it's his turn. We start to eat. The boys are all next to each other on one side, which is probably not a good idea. They're elbowing each other.

[*Lauren's expression suggests mild amusement*]

RICH: Yeah, I can see that happening. What happens next?

[*Lauren's face grows stern.*]

LAUREN: I put my fork down and I just look at them and they stop. But then I smile at them.

RICH: You're tired now and you do not want to put up with that.

LAUREN: No.

RICH: You just got home from work a little while ago. What kind of work do you do?

LAUREN: I work…[*Lauren pauses.*] I don't know if I'm a blacksmith or something like that. Something with metal.

RICH: Do you work close to where you live?

LAUREN: It's in town.

RICH: What town is it?

LAUREN: Sommersville.

RICH: Sommersville. Where is that? What state is that?

LAUREN: Virginia, I think. Yeah, Virginia.

RICH: What year is it?

LAUREN: 1754.

[*Lauren is able to give me great details of this experience, but I am still wondering about the deeper significance of this lifetime. What were the events? What were the lessons? I continue to probe.*]

RICH: Tell me what's happening at dinner. Why is this an important memory? Is there something important that happened?

LAUREN: No, it's just everyday. Mary is telling the children to tell me about their day in school. Sarah had a spelling test; she did very well. She's very smart. And Edward got in trouble and had to stand in the corner.

RICH: How are you feeling?

LAUREN: Good.

[*I continue to wonder where Lauren's higher self is leading us.*]

RICH: You're feeling good. I think it might be good to go to the next important event in this lifetime. Are you ready to do that?

LAUREN: No. Maybe in a minute.

RICH: Okay, then stay where you are. Tell me more about what you are experiencing and what you are enjoying.

LAUREN: The warmth of the fire.

RICH: Mmmm, tell me more.

LAUREN: Mary's food. She is a very good cook. She is a very good mother.

RICH: Did you know her from when you were younger?

LAUREN: Oh, my whole life.

RICH: Was she from the same town?

LAUREN: Yes.

RICH: So you were close friends?

LAUREN: Yes, we were friends growing up. She was the only girl that would get dirty and not get squeamish.

RICH: Just the kind of girl you liked.

LAUREN: Yeah.

RICH: So when did you start going steady?

LAUREN: When we were about sixteen.

RICH: How was that?

LAUREN: Nice. I remember seeing for the first time that she wasn't a tomboy anymore.

RICH: How did that feel?

LAUREN: Great.

RICH: How did she look?

LAUREN: Like an angel.

RICH: Do you remember the first time you kissed?

LAUREN: Yes.

RICH: Tell me about that.

LAUREN: There was a picnic after church and everybody in the town went. We used to go every year. It was like a fall harvest and at night they would have a dance. We always went together as kids because our families always went. Mary was one of the only girls who would play stickball when the other girls…well, I don't know what they always did. (They) sewed, who knows what they did. She was always one of the guys, but that day she wasn't one of the guys. We were allowed to go to the dance because we were older now. I asked her if she would go with me. I asked her father for permission and he said yes. We hung out at the picnic and when her family was getting ready to go home she told me that she would see me later. I told her I would get her around six o'clock and she gave me a kiss on the cheek and then ran off.

RICH: Oh, how did that feel?

LAUREN: Good.

RICH: Very nice. When did you decide to get married?

LAUREN: About a year later.

RICH: How old were you?

LAUREN: Between seventeen and eighteen.

RICH: Very nice. Was it a nice wedding?

LAUREN: Yes. My father was the blacksmith. I worked with him and then when he died, I took over.

RICH: Okay. Are you ready to go to the next important point in this lifetime?

LAUREN: Yes.

RICH: I will count from five to one. When I get to one I will take you to the next important event in this lifetime. I'm going to count down now: Five, four, three, two, one. You are there.

[*Lauren begins to look very sad.*]

RICH: What's going on?

LAUREN: It's a funeral.

RICH: Whose funeral?

LAUREN: Francis.

RICH: Francis, how old was he?

LAUREN: Eight.

RICH: What happened?

LAUREN: He had gotten pneumonia.

RICH: Tell me more.

[*Lauren pauses for a moment.*]

LAUREN: It's after everybody leaves. After the burial.

RICH: What happens?

LAUREN: Mary and I go back home. My mother has the other children.

RICH: Then what happens?

[*Lauren's head tilts downward and her voice is softer.*]

LAUREN: She sits in his spot on the bench.

RICH: Then what happens?

LAUREN: She starts to cry.

RICH: What do you do?

LAUREN: I hold her.

RICH: How are you feeling?

LAUREN: Dead. Helpless.

RICH: How else do you feel?

LAUREN: Angry.

RICH: Angry at whom?

LAUREN: God.

RICH: What do you do?

LAUREN: Nothing. I don't cry.

RICH: Here you are, you've worked hard all your life, had children, had a warm, close, loving family, and you lose Francis. What's the lesson here?

LAUREN: That the dinner I described to you was very important.

[The spirit has now taught both of us a lesson. I continue to affirm out loud].

RICH: Every moment is important.

[I pause a few moments and then I ask for more.]

RICH: What is another lesson?

LAUREN: That you don't have control over everything; that there are things that are out of your hands.

RICH: What should you do about the things that are outside of your control?

LAUREN: You have to accept them. But I don't want to accept this.

RICH: The lesson is that there some are things outside of your control, even if you don't want to accept them. In the meantime, the moments you have together are very important and they are to be treasured.

LAUREN: Yes.

RICH: How does that relate to your current lifetime?

LAUREN: That I can only do what is in my power. Even if I do everything in the ideal way and follow all the rules, there's no guarantee. There are other things, other people's free will; there's just everything in the universe. There's God's plan.

RICH: This is something that you've come to accept.

LAUREN: Yes.

RICH: So you have gained a lot of wisdom and this is part of the reason.

LAUREN: Yes.

RICH: If you are ready to leave this scene I'd like to take you to the very end of this lifetime. Are you ready for that?

LAUREN: Yes.

RICH: I'm going to count from five to one and you're going to be at the very end of this lifetime. Five, four, three, two, one: You are there now, the very end of this lifetime. Be there. Experience it using all of your senses. Is there a glimpse of anything?

LAUREN: I'm in bed.

RICH: How are you feeling?

[*Lauren speaks as if she is weak and out of breath.*]

LAUREN: Old and tired. I don't...I think I had a stroke or something because I don't feel a part of my body.

RICH: How old are you?

LAUREN: Seventy-eight.

RICH: And what part of your body don't you feel?

LAUREN: My legs.

RICH: Both your legs?

LAUREN: Yes.

RICH: Is there anyone with you?

LAUREN: Yes, Mary is there.

RICH: What is happening?

LAUREN: My children are there and their children. And even some of their children.

RICH: So you've raised a large family.

LAUREN: Yes.

RICH: How do you feel?

LAUREN: At rest.

RICH: What happens next?

LAUREN: I want to see the little ones one last time.

RICH: And then what happens?

LAUREN: I look at Mary and she's crying. She still looks the same to me.

RICH: How does she look?

LAUREN: Her hair is white.

RICH: I want you to take one last look at her and look deep into her eyes and into her soul. What do you see?

LAUREN: They are like oceans. Her eyes were always like these two vast beautiful oceans. And I see this woman that I have loved my whole life.

RICH: Okay. The love that you feel for Mary, do you feel that love now, in your current lifetime?

LAUREN: Yes.

RICH: Where do you feel it?

LAUREN: In my family.

RICH: Love is timeless. So you are feeling tired; you are feeling weak.

LAUREN: I'm ready to go.

RICH: You're ready to go. Let me take you right to the end of this lifetime.

LAUREN: Okay.

RICH: I'm going to count again from five to one. When I get to one you will be at the very end of this lifetime. Five, four, three, two, one: You are now at the very end of this lifetime. What's happening?

LAUREN: I hear them talking but it's almost like I am in a tunnel; I can't make out anything, it's very muffled. I can look at them but the hole is getting smaller and smaller. I'm fading, and I'm starting to head toward the light.

RICH: As you are fading and leaving this lifetime and going toward the light...

[*Lauren interrupts me, as her voice gets louder and more excited.*]

LAUREN: Yes, I can turn and it is just white. You can't see walls or anything; it's just this white vastness. There's a pillowy smoke.

RICH: As you are leaving this lifetime do you have any reflections on this lifetime? Were any other important lessons revealed in this lifetime?

LAUREN: I feel like I have had a good life.

RICH: Anything else?

LAUREN: I feel fortunate. I feel proud.

RICH: Anything else?

LAUREN: No.

RICH: So you are leaving this lifetime feeling you've had a good life. You feel fortunate and proud. You were surrounded with a lot of love, the love of a large family. As you go through the tunnel you feel this pure light and gravitate toward it. What happens next?

LAUREN: I see Francis.

RICH: You see Francis?

LAUREN: Yes. He looks exactly the same. I don't feel old. My parents are there and they have their hands on Francis's shoulders. I know that my father had been keeping an eye on him. My mother did, too, after she died.

RICH: How do you feel about that?

LAUREN: Relieved. [*Lauren pauses.*] Mary's parents are there. They are leading me in.

RICH: What happens next?

LAUREN: I go towards them and then all of a sudden, we blend into each other's space. It's not like we are in body form, yet we know each other.

RICH: And then what?

LAUREN: We are floating: Just up.

RICH: How do you feel?

LAUREN: Totally weightless. Every ounce of love that I have ever felt, I am feeling at that very moment all at the same time.

RICH: What a wonderful feeling.

LAUREN: It's a rush.

RICH: It must feel wonderful.

LAUREN: Yes, it does.

RICH: And then what?

LAUREN: I see God.

RICH: Can you describe that more?

LAUREN: It is not an image, just a being, a spirit; I just know it is God.

RICH: What else?

LAUREN: I can see people, again not in body form but I know who they all are.

RICH: Like who?

LAUREN: People I grew up with, people in my family.

RICH: Now that you are in soul form and you have a whole new perspective, what message would you like to send back to those who are in body form?

LAUREN: That this is better than you could ever imagine. You understand everything that you didn't understand before. There is not one bad feeling at all. It's total peace.

[*Lauren looks peaceful. There is a serenity about her that is beyond description.*]

RICH: While you are there do you meet any guardian angels or spirit guides?

LAUREN: I can feel them.

RICH: Do you know their names?

LAUREN: There's a Mary.

RICH: Anyone else?

LAUREN: Timothy.

[*I now decide to start linking Lauren's past life (and death) memory to her present life experience.*]

RICH: Are any of them with you in your *current* lifetime?

LAUREN: Mary is.

RICH: Is she a spirit guide or guardian angel?

LAUREN: I think a spirit guide.

RICH: So Mary is your spirit guide. Is there anyone else you see that is with you in your current lifetime?

LAUREN: I see one that reminds me of my Aunt Sally. I feel that I know her.

RICH: Does she have a name?

LAUREN: Margaret.

RICH: So you have Mary and you have Margaret, and both seem to be around you in this current lifetime. Is there anyone else, any angels? Do you feel the presence of any angels that are with you in this current lifetime?

LAUREN: I see angels.

RICH: What do you see?

LAUREN: I see a girl from my dreams.

RICH: Does she have a name?

LAUREN: Giselle.

RICH: Is she with you in your current lifetime whenever you

need her?

LAUREN: Yes. I never knew her name but yes, she is there. She's the one from my dreams.

RICH: So nice to meet her.

LAUREN: Yes.

RICH: Do you see any angels that are with us in this room?

LAUREN: Giselle is here.

RICH: Anyone else?

LAUREN: I sense my grandfather.

RICH: You have many souls and spirit guides and angels around you all the time. How does that feel?

LAUREN: Comforting.

RICH: Yes. It's a wonderful feeling to know that you are never alone. You have those that surround you in body form and you have those that surround you in spirit form, all the time.

[*Lauren nods.*]

RICH: It's a wonderful, peaceful feeling. Is there anything more that you can gather from this very special place you've found? Any wisdom or messages?

LAUREN: I sense a lot of the Golden Rule.

RICH: Which is?

LAUREN: Treat others the way you want to be treated.

RICH: It's about love.

LAUREN: Yes.

RICH: Love. Loving others the way you like to be loved. It's unconditional love.

LAUREN: To see beyond, I feel there is a message to look beyond people. To look beyond the way people appear on the surface, their race, sex, etc. We are to look instead at their souls. We are to see people as souls. There are wounded souls and there are happy souls. We are supposed to help the wounded souls be happy souls. We are supposed to heal them. That is why we are blessed. That's what we are supposed to do with our blessings.

[*I now decide to help Lauren discover a specific spiritual purpose for her current lifetime.*]

RICH: What is Lauren, in particular, supposed to do in this lifetime? What is Lauren's purpose?

LAUREN: I'm supposed to reach out in many small ways. I'm supposed to do the day-to-day things for others. I'm supposed to do the overlooked things for the sad souls.

RICH: Anything else?

LAUREN: We're supposed to take away the complexity of life and bring everything to (being about) simple basic needs, and then everything else will fall into place.

RICH: You said that we are supposed to do these things?

LAUREN: Everyone. That's what the angels want us all to do.

RICH: Is there anything else that they want us to do?

LAUREN: They want us to feel the power that we all have, that every one of us has the power to do this.

RICH: To do what?

LAUREN: To get rid of the complexity.

RICH: Okay.

LAUREN: Even a child can just smile at someone and make him or her smile back.

RICH: Right.

LAUREN: As parents, that is what we have to teach our children.

RICH: That is a very good lesson. Is there more to share or would you like to come back into the room now?

LAUREN: Come back.

RICH: You're ready to come back?

LAUREN: Yes.

RICH: When we come back I'd like you to keep in mind that there is always love around you. It's always around you in body form and it is always around you in spirit form, giving you love and being there for you. Even after you come into this room, you can have that connection whenever you wish. All you have to do is pause for a few moments, close your eyes, take a few deep breaths, and you can feel the connection. We can always connect with this feeling of peace and relaxation and serenity. We can always rebuild this peace and understanding and be calmer and more joyful than ever before. You take this wisdom that you've experienced in this room with you: It is yours now forever. You can always take this wisdom or this insight with you.

The insight that came from Thomas was the love he shared with his family that he carried right through to his dying day. The insight that came from the heavens where all souls are connected is also always here for you. So, I will gradually awaken you, counting up from one to ten. Know that you will carry this love and sense of peace with you when you come back into this room. As I count from one to ten, with each number you will be more and more awakened and in control of your body. You will be feeling wonderful, great, refreshed, and relaxed. You will be filled with a beautiful, loving energy. Very gradually, very peacefully, I will start to count.

One, two three: You are slowly and gradually awakening, feeling wonderful. Four, five six: feeling more and more awake now, still feeling great. Seven, eight: more and more awake now, very gently, whenever you're ready. Nine, ten: You are gradually getting ready to open your eyes. You have the peace within you. It can last forever.

[*Moments later, Lauren gradually opens her eyes. A few more minutes pass before she is ready to speak.*]

LAUREN: Well that was an amazing experience! It was weird at the end, "good" weird though. When you meet everyone in the white, it is bright as you can imagine, but it doesn't hurt your eyes. There are people to greet you. Like Francis and the parents. You don't feel it but it's like they are pushing you in. Everyone surrounds you and you become one at that point. You know everyone who is there: You don't actually see them but there is a knowingness that they are there. I felt like I was going up, floating, rising.

RICH: Was it a good feeling?

LAUREN: Oh, yeah. Very peaceful, (a) very divine feeling.

You know you are in heaven; there's no sign saying, "Welcome to Heaven," but you know you are there. There are no pearly gates. God is there. You have images of Jesus and Mary (and) there are souls floating around. When your brain makes that recognition, you then put the face on that soul.

RICH: Sure, the recognition of souls.

LAUREN: What struck me was that when you asked me their names, their names were ones that I have been drawn to my whole life. I thought of naming my daughter Kayla "Mary" at one point. It's also my mother's name but I felt another pull toward it. "Thomas" was the boy name I had for Kayla. "James" was the boy name I had for my other daughter, Brianna.

RICH: It's an association with a memory.

LAUREN: Yes, that's exactly what it is. You just don't know it at the time.

RICH: Oh sure.

LAUREN: As a woman, the kind of man that Thomas was is the kind of man you fantasize about. People say it doesn't exist; they blame it on watching *Cinderella*. There is this knowing that yes, this type of man exists. There are men that love their wives deeply. And while back then, women had no rights and there were societal things, Thomas did respect Mary.

RICH: So what you are saying is that you know there are men like that because *you* were a man like that?

LAUREN: Yes. Until I knew this, I just had this feeling deep inside me that men can be this way. Now I know why.

RICH: So what does this realization mean about the man you are now married to?

LAUREN: Chris is a great guy and I love him very much. But now I can see why I sometimes get very frustrated with him. He is often so busy with work and he comes home so tired that I sometimes feel neglected by him. I know it's not intentional, but it still bothers me.

RICH: What do you say to him when you're feeling

neglected?

LAUREN: I tell him we need to talk, or I tell him we don't have enough quality time, or something like that.

RICH: And what does he say?

LAUREN: He's usually busy with something and asks me to wait until later, which never seems to come. Or he tells me that we have plenty of quality time and that I'm just looking for a problem. Or sometimes he gets defensive and says I'm overly sensitive and moody because I must be getting my period.

RICH: So now what is going to be different?

LAUREN: Now I know I'm not crazy. I know what I feel. I know that when I need him to put his projects aside and come to dinner, it's because I need to feel more connected to him. And when I want him to sit with me after dinner and have a simple conversation with me about what is going on with him and me and our family, I shouldn't think that I am bothering him too much.

RICH: That's true.

LAUREN: Now I know that the simple things are what we need to focus on more, in order to appreciate the love that we share.

RICH: Definitely.

LAUREN: And since now I know that I was a man in a past life who could appreciate all the love a family has to offer, I know I'm not asking too much from Chris right now.

RICH: How does it feel to have connected with your soul on a very deep and personal level? And how do you feel about the notion that there are possible spirit guides and angels around you?

LAUREN: I've always felt them around me. I just never talked much about it.

RICH: And now you have names.

LAUREN: Yes. Giselle is my guardian angel. She is always there. It is something that I have always believed in but now I do even more, and even deeper. [Lauren pauses to reflect further.] Those messages about keeping things simple: We hear them all the time and say, yes, yes, yes, but we get caught up in the complexities of life.

RICH: Right, the business of life.

LAUREN: When we lose ourselves in our jobs and work and forget these little things in life, that's when crisis sets in. These little things: They are very important.

RICH: We can't lose our perspective.

LAUREN: Little simple things (like) holding a door for someone, smiling, saying good morning, etc. For a while, I have been feeling that life is not as meaningful as it should be. I have been thinking about what the purpose of my life is. That's when I first thought about coming to see you. Now after this experience, I know it has to do with helping people. How that will happen, I don't know yet. But I do know that while I'm raising my two girls, I would like to start helping people through the little hurdles in life. I'm not going to cure diseases, but I can start doing little things, like giving blood.

RICH: It all counts.

LAUREN: It definitely counts to the person who *gets* the blood. These small little things that don't take much effort are what we are supposed to do. I am to plant some seeds, give little nudges, and encourage people to do these things.

RICH: All the little things are expressions of love, compassion, and ways we can each reaffirm our deeper connection to one another.

LAUREN: Exactly.

RICH: So as we end our session, is there anything more you would like to add?

LAUREN: Just that this was probably the most amazing experience I've ever had. I came to see you not because of any particular problem I could put my finger on. I came because I thought that this past life regression experience might help me understand why I was feeling generally dissatisfied or lost lately. It wasn't something I could explain to anyone, except maybe to my friend Debbie, who used to see you.

RICH: Well, I don't think it was any coincidence that Debbie happened to share her experience with you around the same time you needed to hear about it.

LAUREN: I agree. In fact, I think somehow Giselle got that conversation started between us that day.

For Lauren, there would have been no other way to arrive at this discovery and resolution. Her underlying sadness and dissatisfaction with her life did not have its source in her present. Traditional psychotherapy was able to address only some of her feelings, those that were linked to her recent childhood experiences and memories. In Lauren's case, the hurt went back further than that.

I ran into Lauren six months later in a local bookstore. The brightness in her eyes and the serenity in her smile confirmed to me that she is indeed a much happier woman than she was before the regression experience. Discovering and understanding the source of her feelings in a previous life experience made it possible for her to identify and resolve them in the present.

I am certain that I have been here as I am now a thousand times before,
and I hope to return a thousand times.
—Johann Wolfgang von Goethe
(German writer, philosopher and diplomat)

Case Study B

Finding The Missing Pieces: Healing the Wounds of Sexual Abuse

*Our inner guidance comes to us through our feelings
and body wisdom first—not through intellectual understanding…
The intellect works best in service to our intuition,
our inner guidance, soul, God or higher power.*

—Christiane Northrup

"**I** think I need to come back for a counseling session," said Paula on the phone. "But this time, I would like to come just for myself."

Paula and Bobby had come to my office just over a year earlier for marriage counseling (as detailed in my first book, *Turning Trauma Into Triumph*). At that time, Paula was imploding with suppressed secrets of sexual abuse. She realized that holding onto painful memories bound her up emotionally and physically. She needed to acknowledge and address her history of sexual abuse before she could reclaim and exclaim her personal power.

"I found a lot of relief after last year," explained Paula in my office, "and it helped me to articulate and assert my needs to Bobby. He has been great and our relationship has been much better, but lately I've been thinking that maybe there's something more."

"More?" I asked. "What do you mean?"

"Well, it seems we were able to go over everything that happened to me, going all the way back to junior high school."

"Yes, I remember."

Paula had been verbally and sexually assaulted by a fellow student in a stairwell at school. When she reported the incident to the principal, the trauma of the attack was further intensified by the principal's insensitive and dismissive response. After questioning Paula's attacker, he suggested that perhaps Paula had just *led the poor fellow on.* Not only had Paula felt violated, but she had been made to feel responsible for it as well.

"But what if there was something that happened even before junior high school?"

"Why would you think that? You never mentioned anything before about any other memories of abuse."

"Yeah, I know. There aren't any other memories. I mean, I have thought about it a lot and I can't think of anything else that might have happened. So logically, I tell myself to stop dwelling on it already. But emotionally, I can't stop feeling that there is some big chunk missing."

"A big chunk?"

"Yeah, a big chunk. That's the only way I can describe it."

"Do you have any idea what this big chunk may consist of?"

"Well, yes. One part that I think about and I don't quite understand is why I was so compliant so often."

"What do you mean?"

"I'm thinking about Matt. I remember it like it was yesterday. I mean, even after the guy raped me, I continued to date him for a few more months. That was crazy. Why would I do that?"

"Well, I don't think it was so crazy. When we had gone over that whole episode, you were very clear that you somehow felt guilty and responsible for some of what had happened. You thought that somehow you may have led him on and that it was possibly your fault that he could not hold back from having sex with you. You also had very low self-esteem at that time, and you believed that maybe you owed him sex because that was all you were good for."

Paula began to cry. "I know. That's all true; it's terrible to have felt that way. That's why I'm so glad you were able to help me deal with all that crap."

"So…do you still think there's more?"

"Yes, sometimes I still do. When I think back, I remember that most of my friends were very unsure of themselves. I remember that they all would talk about guys that were nice and guys that were mean. A lot of my friends put up with stuff that they shouldn't have. But I can't imagine any of them putting up with what I put up with. It was beyond low self-esteem. It was just an overwhelming feeling of 'this is the way it was (and) you just had to live with it or you would be left completely alone.' I was just too quiet about it. My attitude about it was too self-defeating."

"Okay, you know how you feel better than I do. So if there really is something more left to be uncovered, there are a few ways to look for it."

"Okay, I'm listening."

"Well, you said the only clue you have is an overwhelming feeling that haunts you about your experience."

"That's right."

"Do you have any glimpse of a scene that may go with that memory?"

"Like a flashback?"

"Like anything. It could be visual or it could be a very uncomfortable feeling associated with something you have heard. Or maybe a smell or something you have touched."

"No, I can't think of anything at all."

"Well, we could try hypnosis."

"Hypnosis?"

"Yes. I could help you get into a deeply relaxing trance that would help you focus on any deep memories that you may have that you're not fully conscious of."

"Yes, we talked about hypnosis the last time we worked together. I think I would like to try that."

"As we discussed earlier, we can use the hypnosis to go as far back as you would like. I would purposely not suggest you go back to any particular age; I would let you or your higher self pick out a time to remember."

"Do you think I could remember any past life experience, also? I remember talking to you about it at the time. I was fascinated with the idea, but I wasn't ready to try it. After all, there was so much going on with my current life at the time."

"That's for sure. To answer your question, we can do whatever you want. This is your time."

"Well, I really want to try it. I'm not afraid anymore. I have to find out what this feeling is all about."

"I just want to remind you: There is a good chance you may not recall any past life memory the first time you try. In fact, I don't know if you will be able to recover any other early childhood memory, since you have to be ready and able to be hypnotized before you will accept my suggestion to recall anything."

"Well, I think I'm as ready as I'll ever be."

"Okay, we'll try next week if you like."

"Great, I'll be ready."

The following week, Paula arrived at my office ready for her adventure. She did not appear to be anxious or apprehensive at all. I was confident that she was ready for a good experience.

"Once again, I want to remind you that we will work together and give it our best shot. If you don't recover any memory of your childhood or a past life, that's okay. It may be that a nice, two-hour experience of being deeply relaxed is all that happens today and that's okay, because that's also a wonderful experience that most people never have."

"Yes, I understand. Whatever happens is okay with me."

"I will also remind you that what I suggest is *only* a suggestion. You always have the choice whether or not to follow that suggestion. You are always in control. If you find yourself in a place that is uncomfortable, you always have the choice of reexperiencing the scene from a distance, by imagining that you are floating above the scene and witnessing your experience with less intensity. Or you can choose to reexperience a memory fully, using all of your senses."

"Yes, I remember you explaining this to me."

"And of course, you can choose to move away from a memory totally if you wish. It is always up to you."

"Yes."

"And once again, be assured that you will remember every part of the experience that you will report to me. In fact, you will remember more of the experience than you have time to describe."

"What do you mean?"

"Well, if you are able to recover graphic memories, it will involve most of your senses: sight, sound, touch, smell, etc. It's like being in the middle of Disney World and then calling me on the phone to describe what it is you're experiencing. There is so much going on, you'll only be able to describe a portion of it. You'll remember the rest of the experience, but I'll only know the part you were able to report to me."

"Okay, I get it."

"So are you ready?"

"Yes, I'm ready."

"Then I want you to start by getting yourself in a nice comfortable position, either sitting up or lying down. Whichever you prefer."

"Okay."

"Then I would like you to close your eyes and start to take some nice, slow, deep breaths, and just do that for a few moments. As you focus on your breaths—these slow deep breaths—let yourself go deeper and deeper and deeper into a relaxed, serene, tranquil state."

Paula had no problem reaching a deep level of peace and relaxation. Moments later, she transitioned easily into a light hypnotic state. Soon, she was able to recall and reexperience a very detailed memory of being with her older sister, Suzanne.

Suzanne was reading her a bedtime story when she was four

years old. It was a very tender, loving time in Paula's life. She described not only the pastel painted walls and woven throw rug, but she detailed exactly the pajamas she and Suzanne were wearing that special evening. It was a wonderful live snapshot demonstrating the bond that was being established between the two of them. It was a very important memory.

Soon I helped Paula transition to an experience at a younger age. She and her cousin Frankie were playing with blocks in the living room of her old house. It was a very light, fun, and carefree time of her life. It is another very important memory. It reinforced warmer, more loving feelings that on a very deep level are hers to hold and cherish for a lifetime. We are ready to proceed even further.

I begin the process of past life regression:

RICH: Do you want to stay with this memory or do you want to go further?

PAULA: Further.

RICH: You're ready to go further?

PAULA: Yes.

RICH: Now you will be able to go deep inside yourself and remember everything. You can remember every experience you've ever had. You can go back as far as you wish. You can go back in this lifetime, or you may choose to recall a memory from a previous lifetime. Let yourself experience, let yourself remember...You are now totally inside this new place, or new space. This new place or space might be inside or it might be outside. As the images before you become clearer, you will start to experience something new.

[*A few moments pass.*]

RICH: Do you have any sense of where you might be?

PAULA: It's like a cellar.

RICH: A cellar?

PAULA: Yes. It's dark.

[*Paula starts to grimace.*]

PAULA: It smells.

RICH: Smells like?

PAULA: Urine. It's disgusting! There are rats.

[*Paula* looks *disgusted.*]

RICH: How are you feeling?

PAULA: Sick.

RICH: What hurts?

[*Paula leans forward a bit.*]

PAULA: I feel sick to my stomach. I have a feeling…I'm not, like, scared, but it is a feeling of dread. I've been here before.

RICH: How do you know that?

PAULA: Because I know he's coming.

RICH: You know *he's* coming. Who is coming?

[*Paula's face scowls vehemently.*]

PAULA: A man. I *hate* him.

RICH: What does he want?

PAULA: [*Pauses briefly.*] He *owns* me.

RICH: Is he coming soon?

PAULA: Yes, that is why they put me in the dungeon.

RICH: And how are you feeling now?

[*Paula shakes her head from side to side.*]

PAULA: I just want to get it over with. I wish he would die. I hope he trips on the steps and breaks his neck!

RICH: What is he like?

[*Paula's nostrils flare.*]

PAULA: He *smells.* He's old and fat. He has no teeth. He's disgusting!

RICH: What is his name?

PAULA: Everett.

RICH: Is he coming soon?

PAULA: He will be.

RICH: What do you do in the meantime?

[*Paula's voice quiets down.*]

PAULA: I don't do anything.

RICH: You just wait. Are you alone or is there someone else

with you?

PAULA: I'm alone.

RICH: Is it light there or is it dark?

PAULA: It is light outside. There's a small window by the ceiling. It's daytime, but there are some candles lit because it is dark down here. It's musty: It's the wine cellar. There are bottles of wine.

RICH: What happens next?

PAULA: I hear footsteps. I'm under the kitchen; there are lots of footsteps. Lots of noise, pots and pans. I hear muffled talking.

RICH: Who is upstairs?

PAULA: The others.

RICH: Who are the others?

PAULA: My cousins—a couple of cousins—and my mother. They are in the kitchen, even Everett's wife.

RICH: Everett's wife?

PAULA: Yes.

RICH: What happens next?

[*Paula speaks softly.*]

PAULA: I'm praying that it just gets over (with). I want it to be over with.

RICH: What happens next?

PAULA: He's coming. They have stopped talking.

RICH: They stopped talking upstairs?

PAULA: Yeah. He's in the kitchen. They know.

RICH: They know he's coming down?

PAULA: Yes. He does it to them, too.

[*I pause to think about what has just been said. I am a little apprehensive about the direction that this experience is taking, but I know that Paula's higher power has decided that Paula needs to reexperience this event for a greater purpose. I have faith that Spirit knows better than I about what Paula needs right now. With confidence, I continue to probe forward.*]

RICH: What happens next?

PAULA: I hear the door squeaking. It's one of those doors

on the floor. He's coming. I want to *kill* him. I'm going to kill him sometime.

RICH: He's a very mean man. He's coming down.

PAULA: Yes.

RICH: What happens next?

[*Paula's voice gets loud and she appears disgusted once again.*]

PAULA: He's drunk. He stinks.

[*I decide to diffuse the event for a moment, and I ask Paula for more information.*]

RICH: What is your name?

PAULA: Lizzie.

RICH: Do you have a last name?

PAULA: No. I'm just Lizzie.

RICH: How old are you?

PAULA: I don't know. I guess I'm about fifteen.

RICH: So he's coming down the cellar, this wine cellar. Where is this house?

PAULA: On a farm. A little fancy, (but) not real fancy.

RICH: Do you know what state you are in?

PAULA: No.

RICH: Okay.

PAULA: We don't have to know those things.

RICH: What do you look like?

PAULA: I have dark hair and dark skin.

RICH: What are you wearing?

PAULA: A long cotton dress, an apron, and a cloth hat.

RICH: What year is it?

PAULA: I don't know.

RICH: What would you guess?

PAULA: Early 1800s. It's like a small plantation. It's not very big.

[*I now decide to return to the experience. I know it is very important.*]

RICH: So he's on his way down. What happens? What happens

next?

PAULA: He stops; he's almost at the end of the stairs and he just stops. He's got a bottle of something and he drinks from it. He has greasy hair. He's sweaty. He just has a stupid-ass grin on his face.

RICH: Then what happens?

PAULA: He points. There's a cot with straw on it in the corner. He just points.

RICH: What does that mean?

[*Paula growls as she speaks.*]

PAULA: It's time. I have to lie on the bed.

RICH: What do you do?

[*Paula continues to growl and grimace.*]

PAULA: I do it. The last time I didn't want to and he hit me with his belt.

RICH: So this time you do it?

PAULA: That's what everyone says, (to) just get it over with. There is no use fighting him. One time I'm gonna kill him.

RICH: So you hate him.

PAULA: I hate him! He did this to my mother, to my sister, and my cousins.

RICH: These are all girls, your cousins?

PAULA: The ones in the kitchen.

RICH: They are all girls?

PAULA: Yes. The boys are out in the fields. My cousins and my sister are house-workers.

[*I return to Lizzie's experience. I know that every detail is very important.*]

RICH: So this time you decide to just get it over with like you were told.

PAULA: Yes.

RICH: So you go to lie on the bed.

PAULA: Yes.

RICH: What happens next?

PAULA: He undoes his pants. I just lie there and close my eyes.

RICH: And then what happens?

PAULA: He starts to rape me. He warns me not to fight him or he'll do what he did last time.

RICH: What do you do?

PAULA: I cry. [*Paula pauses.*] He killed one of us. He killed another girl. He made us watch.

RICH: How did he do that?

PAULA: She tried to run away. She was fighting him. She tried to get away and she made it up the stairs. I was in the kitchen with my mother and one of my cousins. We were cooking. Kimmie got up; her dress was all torn and she was bleeding. He grabbed her by the hair and he threw her into the wall. He took her hand and he stuck it on the stove. We weren't allowed to help her or he'd beat us, too. And he threw hot water on her and she was screaming. Then he left and we helped her. We got cold water and Mamma looked at her hand. [*Paula pauses again and her voice gets softer.*] The next day he killed her. [*Paula starts to cry.*]

RICH: How are you feeling?

PAULA: Sad.

RICH: What do you do with that sadness?

[*Paula's voice gets loud once again.*]

PAULA: I hate him!

RICH: So you don't feel it; you turn it into anger.

PAULA: Yes.

RICH: You refuse to feel sad.

PAULA: If I do, he wins.

RICH: When you feel sad, he wins.

PAULA: That's what he wants.

RICH: When you feel sad, that's a very strong feeling that you have.

PAULA: Yes.

[*I decide that it's time to link this past life memory to Paula's current lifetime experience.*]

RICH: Is that connected with your life *today?*

PAULA: Yes.

RICH: How is it connected?

PAULA: I couldn't cry growing up. I had to swallow it. I had to take it.

RICH: And you do that well. When you do that in this lifetime, what happens?

PAULA: I get a lot of anxiety. [*Paula starts to feel anxious. Her body begins to tremble.*] I want to leave this [*she says abruptly*].

RICH: Okay, we can leave this. [*As always I respect her wishes.*] Do you want to go to the end of this lifetime? Do you want to float above?

PAULA: [*Still crying*] I just want to leave it.

RICH: Okay, we can do that. I'm going to count from ten to one and you will be able to leave this lifetime. Ten, nine, eight, seven, six, five, four, three, two, one. You are no longer experiencing this lifetime. You are safe.

[*Paula instantly relaxes. She sighs. Her breathing becomes full and rhythmic. Her body and face show a sense of deep peace. I continue.*]

RICH: You've gained rich insight. You've had a very intense experience, but you are safe now. I can understand why it might have been safe to suppress your feelings—that's what you needed to do to survive—but now you are safe. You don't need to suppress your feelings any longer. However you feel is okay. All of your feelings are beautiful and important. You are safe now. What happened to Lizzie was a long time ago. In this lifetime you are safe to have and express your feelings. You never have to change your feelings to please anyone. You never have to change your feelings (into) either anger or anxiety. You can just have your feelings the way they are. You are safe now. It was a very important insight to know why feelings are a hindrance to you. Locating the source of this pain is healing. You are now safe and you can relax. Take deep breaths. You feel safe and you can just sit and rest.

[*I pause a few more moments. Paula continues to relax. Once again,
I ask Paula's higher self what she wants to do.*]

RICH: You have the choice to take another journey, to meet a
spirit guide...

[*Paula interrupts me.*]

PAULA: They are there now.

[*I don't know what Paula is referring to, but I prompt her to tell me
more.*]

RICH: They are there now?

PAULA: I am embracing them.

RICH: Tell me.

PAULA: My grandfather is here and Deena and Jack are here.

[*I know that Deena and Jack are relatives of Paula's that passed on
when Paula was much younger.*]

RICH: What's happening?

PAULA: We are on the hammock.

RICH: So you are on the hammock, and your grandfather is
there and Jack and Deena are there.

PAULA: Yes.

RICH: Very nice. Are you swinging?

PAULA: A little.

RICH: Tell me more.

PAULA: I'm leaning on my grandfather. He has his arms around
me from behind. Jack and Deena are on either side of us, embracing
us. They were there waiting for me as I entered a garden.

RICH: So you entered a garden with them?

PAULA: Yes.

RICH: So they are always there for you.

PAULA: Yes.

RICH: They are with you at all times. Very nice. They love you
and are always there for you. They are there to hold you whenever
you need them to.

[*I want to make every effort to help Paula use this experience as
a positive reminder that she is safe to acknowledge and express her*

feelings openly, whenever she chooses. While she remains in a suggestive hypnotic state, I repeat several affirmations to her, over and over, as if I'm chanting.]

RICH: You can enjoy this comfort whenever you choose. As you enjoy it, continue to breathe deep. And have your feelings. You can have your feelings now. It's safe from now on to have your feelings. You can be sad or you can be angry. You can feel happy; you can feel whatever you want. You are restored. You are healed. You are in a new place. You have a craving to be yourself; you are no one's slave. You own yourself. You have free will to do as you please. You can choose to be and feel what you want to. So as you rock in your hammock, you are being embraced by your grandfather and by Deena and Jack. Allow yourself to just take it all in and enjoy that. You never have to be afraid again. You have the power. You never have to be afraid of anyone else nor afraid of having these feelings. You are always free to be yourself, to be happy, to be angry, to be sad, to cry; it is your right. It is your freedom. It is your spirit. Even long after this session, if you forget, (even) for a moment, all you need to do is close your eyes for a second and you will remember that. You never have to be afraid again.

[*Paula now appears deeply relaxed and peaceful. She has a warm, contented smile on her face. Once again, I ask Paula's higher self for the direction she wants to take.*]

RICH: We can stay here longer if you wish or whenever you are ready, you can choose to return to this room.

PAULA: I am ready to return to the room.

RICH: Okay then. Very gradually I'm going to count from one to ten. As I count you will gradually come back into this room. But before I awaken you, I want to remind you that you will be able to recall every part of the experience you have had tonight. You will recall not only the memories of your past life, but you will also recall all the insight and wisdom you have obtained. You know that you have recalled a very difficult experience. But you are also now aware that serenity, peace, and relaxation are always here to be gotten. There is no situation that you cannot overcome. Now you have the wisdom and power and the self-confidence. You are filled with peace and love.

After the regression experience, Paula and I discussed the deep meaning of it all. Paula realized that the sexual part of her that was fearful in this lifetime resonated with the haunting traumatic events that she had experienced in a previous lifetime. The feeling of not being safe sexually was so intense that Paula's body remembered the trauma through this lifetime.

"Does it make sense that I can *feel* something in my body that I can't understand mentally?"

"Definitely. There is a theory that deep memories are reflected more in your body than in your mind. Some people call it cellular memory. That is why your posture will often give more clues about something that happened to you than anything you may say."

"Now that I know what happened to Lizzie, everything makes a little more sense to me. I can see now that if something bad did happen to me, it happened a long, long time ago, and I don't have to worry about it now. It's hard to explain, but I just *feel* better."

After our session ended, Paula left my office with a sense that she had resolved a very ancient dilemma. She had spent several months in therapy trying to gain her sexual freedom, and this experience seemed to explain the last piece of the puzzle. As Paula walked out of my office, I reminded her that she might have more thoughts or dreams in the coming week.

When Paula entered my office a week later, she was excited to give me an update about her regression experience. Apparently, Paula had had a very graphic dream about Lizzie the same night she left my office:

"I dreamed about Lizzie and about what happened after he raped her."

"So, what happened?"

"A few weeks later, she was working in the kitchen, fixing his dinner."

"Go on."

"He had started to go after Lizzie's younger sister and cousin. He took them both down to the cellar, you know, to rape them too."

"And then what happened?"

"Lizzie was enraged. I mean she was furious. There was no way in hell that she was going to let that shit happen to her little sister and cousin!"

"What did she do?"

"She decided to end things once and for all!"

"End things?"

"Yes. Lizzie went to the cupboard and took the poison that they used to kill the rats and she mixed a bunch of it into his soup."

"Then what happened?"

"She waited until he was done downstairs and served him his supper."

"And?"

"She watched him eat every last drop of that soup. A little while later, while the bastard was smoking his pipe, he keeled over, clutching his chest. Lizzie was the only one nearby. She watched him die right in front of her."

"Then what did she do?"

"After a few minutes, she started yelling for help. You know, for appearances. She said that she went into the room to bring him his ale and he was lying on the floor."

"So, how did she feel?"

"Part of her felt a little guilty. But honestly, she felt that he had it coming to him. In fact, she felt really good. She finally felt *empowered*."

"And how do *you* feel?"

"I felt some relief for her. She finally had some control over her life. You know, I've been thinking about Lizzie all week. I really *like* her. She was a very strong woman. I feel that she is still a part of me."

"She is."

"Yes. And I feel much stronger now."

Paula's dream experience was a greater affirmation than I could have ever suggested under hypnosis. Paula's higher power and underlying spirit helped her regain a sense of conviction and strength that she had never experienced before, at least in her current lifetime. Paula was no longer haunted by what she called a big chunk of sadness, of something missing in her life that she could not explain. She now felt whole. She now felt healed.

...It is absolutely necessary that the soul should be healed and purified,
and if this does not take place during its life on earth,
it must be accomplished in future lives.
—St. Gregory (early Christian; 257-332 A.D.)

Case Study C

A Soul's Reunion: Coping with Grief and Loss

There are only two ways to live your life:
One is as though nothing is a miracle.
The other is as though everything is a miracle.
I prefer the latter.

—Albert Einstein

"Thank you for agreeing to see Mark," said Sandy on the phone. "He's in pretty bad shape since being injured in the World Trade Center. But they're planning to release him in a few weeks. He's going to need someone to help him sort this out."

"I'm glad that I'm here to help," I replied. "I'll do my best to help him get past this whole ordeal."

"I know it's not going to be easy. He's still in a lot of pain and they say he'll need more surgery and rehabilitation over the next few years. I'm just glad I still have him," Sandy continued, holding back her tears.

"Yes," I agreed. "There are no words to describe the whole mess. We have *all* been traumatized by this event."

"You know, I was thinking," Sandy continued. "In the past month, everyone has been calling to ask how Mark is doing. It's very nice, but I'm having a very hard time repeating the whole story over and over again. It's like I'm reliving that day each time someone asks questions like, 'What floor did he work on? How did he get out? How bad are the burns? Can he move his fingers?' Oh my God, Rich, I know they all mean well but it's really getting to me. I think I may need to come see you myself."

Whenever I consider treating both partners on an individual basis, I am especially sensitive to the importance of client confidentiality. As such, I never share what either one has to say to me in session. Despite this firm position, I recognize the possibility that this arrangement may be a cause for concern for one or both clients. Therefore, I always offer the alternative of another therapist to treat one of them. I explained the possible conflicts and the options to Sandy.

"Well, I actually mentioned it to Mark last night," she responded, "and we would both rather just see *you*."

"Alright, that's fine," I replied, "but if there comes a time where it seems that either one of you may be holding something back because you're afraid about it being completely confidential, we'll have to deal with it right away."

Sandy agreed, and we made plans to meet for her first individual session the following week. When she arrived in my office, I could see the stress in her face and the worry in her eyes. She sat quietly for a moment, staring at her hands folded in her lap. I asked her to tell me about how things were going for her now.

"Mark always took care of the finances," explained Sandy. "He knew about all of our accounts and how much to pay on each bill every month. In fact, he used to handle it all online from his laptop at work. Since he had an hour every day for lunch, he took care of all that stuff."

"Now that Mark is in the hospital and all our financial records are lost," Sandy continued, "I have to call everyone up to find out if I owe them money and how much I have to pay. I also don't know what Mark's company is going to do about his pay. I don't even know if he'll ever be able to work again. If he has to go on permanent disability, I don't know how we'll be able to live."

Sandy and I reviewed the practical problems at length, while I tried to help her cope with the emotional fallout of this event.

"I'm also worried about my daughter. She looks very upset, but she keeps telling me she's okay. I just don't believe it. She just started her senior year of high school."

"Well, I'm sure this has affected her greatly as well," I responded, "but I'm sure that she may worry that she might add more to your burden. So it seems that she is going to try to cope with this as well as she can *without* your help." In addition, I explained, "Going back to school and trying to resume some kind of normal daily routine may be what's best for her now. It may be that the best you can do is to remind her that if she needs to talk this out with a counselor, I'm sure that I can help find her the right person."

Last but not least, Sandy had to discuss how best to help her husband adjust from being a company executive and family leader to someone who is traumatized and physically disabled. Part of Mark's mandate to start healing emotionally was to address the feelings associated with his trauma openly. Mark *needed* to talk about 9/11 on a daily basis. He needed to piece together every minute of that day so that he could start to make some sense of it for himself. Mark also needed to verbalize and externalize all the trauma and fear associated with the event, in order to start feeling a sense of control over the chaos of that day. As a result, Mark repeated the horrors of his experience over and over to each person he met after leaving the hospital. And with each retelling of his personal ordeal, Mark felt a little more control over his emotions. He felt a little clearer about his new place in the world, and hoped to develop a better idea as to what may come next.

In contrast, Sandy needed a break from hearing her husband retell his story over and over again. Sandy needed to find peace by detaching from her husband for short periods of time. She needed to reclaim her life as one that was separate from her public role as the dutiful wife of a 9/11 survivor. Sandy needed to recover her own *identity*—the one that existed before 9/11—and the one that was determined to have hope for the future.

Over the next few months, Sandy and I talked about issues above and beyond her husband and her daughters. In the course of these discussions, I discovered that Sandy was a very spiritual person who wondered why this event had happened to her and her family.

I learned that this was not the only tragedy that Sandy had suffered in her life. She had questioned why God "allowed bad things to happen to good people." So many things happened to her that didn't seem to make sense or serve any purpose. If indeed God "had a plan for her," Sandy needed to know what exactly it was that she was supposed to learn from these experiences.

"The last time I hurt this much was about twenty-five years ago, when Mark and I were first married," explained Sandy. "I had gotten pregnant and we were very excited to be having our first baby. Everything seemed to be going fine throughout all nine months. We got his room ready and we picked out a name for him." Sandy paused for a moment and took a deep breath. "Then I went to the doctor a few days before my due date for a routine checkup. But the doctor couldn't find a heartbeat. After he examined me completely, he told me that the baby had died." Sandy started to cry.

Sandy had to carry her dead child in her womb before labor could be induced. When her son was finally born, the baby was quickly taken away before Sandy had a chance to hold him. There was no funeral. There was no formal acknowledgment of her worst nightmare. There was no time or place to mourn for her loss.

She sank into a deep depression. Months later, she decided to leave that house and that town and try to make a fresh start somewhere else. Mark was also devastated, and both agreed to relocate to another part of Long Island. The move helped somewhat, but Sandy continued to be haunted by the trauma of losing her son, especially around the anniversary of his death.

During several of our sessions, Sandy told me about watching John Edward's television show, *Crossing Over*.

"You know, I also read two of his books," confided Sandy. "I believe that what he says is true. I really think that he can talk to the spirits of people who have died."

"Yes, I've seen the show," I responded. "It *does* seem pretty amazing."

"So you believe it's true?" she asked.

"Well, to tell you the truth," I explained, "John actually grew up on Long Island. I happen to know people who knew him when he was just starting out doing readings. I also happen to have had clients who got personal readings from him *before* he got famous. And they have all told me that he was very accurate about some unusual details regarding themselves or the person who had died, so each of them was very convinced he is for real."

"Well, I keep praying to God for some answers," added Sandy. "Sometimes I wish I could get an appointment with someone like him myself."

Sandy's open-minded approach to spirituality and her powerful desire to understand what was happening to her made me confident that a past life regression session could help her find some of the answers she was seeking. When I discussed the idea with Sandy, she was very excited about embarking on this spiritual adventure. So we set up an extended appointment time for the following week.

Sandy arrived at my office both relaxed and excited, and she was able to go into a trance without any difficulty. She was able to reexperience two episodes from her early childhood. With her eyes closed, a big smile accompanied her reports of simple and wonderful remembrances.

Then I suggested that she could move to an earlier memory, possibly one that took place at a time before she was born. I asked Sandy if she had a glimpse of something visual or of something that she smelled, heard, sensed, or felt. This time, Sandy just recalled feeling anxious.

I questioned her:

RICH: Anxious?

SANDY: Yeah, I am feeling anxious. I have a sense that something is going to happen.

RICH: Where are you?

SANDY: I am in a closed space. It is rather dark.

RICH: It's dark?

[*Sandy pauses for a moment.*]

SANDY: I'm in a house and there is a wood-burning stove—it's black, tall, and hot. I can feel the heat. There is a pipe that comes out of the stove and goes into the wall. There are clothes hanging in this room.

RICH: Yes.

SANDY: There's a rope hung; there are children's mittens on this rope.

RICH: Can you tell me more about the room you are in?

SANDY: It's a small room, but it is warm.

RICH: Can you describe the floor?

SANDY: There is a hook rug. It is pink and blue with other different colors.

RICH: What kind of floor is it?

SANDY: It's wood, but it is not cold. There are thin pieces of wood with pine knots in them.

RICH: So, what kind of house is this?

[*Sandy begins to describe the house slowly.*]

SANDY: Well, it's a house but it's *not* a house.

[*I thought about this silently for a moment. I decided to seek further clarification.*]

RICH: I want you to go out the door and turn around.

SANDY: Okay.

RICH: Now tell me what you see.

[*Sandy's eyebrows rise up in surprise.*]

SANDY: Oh, it's an igloo! The door is *round* on top. It is white and it is very cold outside but it's also rather dark outside.

[*Sandy's shoulders rise up and she seems to be getting chilled.*]

RICH: If you're cold you can go back into the house and get warm.

SANDY: Okay.

RICH: Is there anyone else in this house?

[*Sandy's eyes search back and forth underneath her eyelids.*]

SANDY: No, I don't see anyone.

RICH: So, how do you feel?

SANDY: I feel okay.

RICH: Does anyone else live in this house?

SANDY: Yes.

RICH: Can you tell me about the other people?

SANDY: [*Pauses a moment.*] I'm the mother!

RICH: Okay. So do you have children?

SANDY: Yes, I do. [*Sandy has a proud look on her face.*] In fact, those mittens are *my girl's* mittens!

RICH: Oh. Where is she?

SANDY: The children are at school.

RICH: Hold old is your daughter?

SANDY: She's four years old.

RICH: How many children do you have?

[*Sandy smiles.*]

SANDY: I have three.

RICH: Can you tell me about your other children?

SANDY: I have a boy who is fifteen and another boy who is twelve.

RICH: Can you tell me *more* about your children? Can you describe your daughter?

SANDY: She's blonde.

RICH: What about your fifteen-year-old?

SANDY: He's got brown hair and he's tall.

RICH: How about your twelve-year-old?

[*Sandy pauses for a moment. Then her smile disappears and she suddenly appears very serious.*]

SANDY: He's not here!

RICH: What do you mean?

SANDY: I'm a little worried.

RICH: Where are the children?

SANDY: My older boy and my daughter are just coming home from school. But my twelve-year-old is not here!

RICH: And how worried are you?

SANDY: I'm *very* upset. I can feel my heart beating and I'm starting to get very worried.

[*Sandy's chest rises and her breathing becomes shallower.*]

RICH: How are your other children feeling right now?

SANDY: They're teasing each other.

RICH: How do they feel?

SANDY: They are not worried.

[*I pursue Sandy's concern.*]

RICH: What happens next?

SANDY: I'm really starting to get upset and I don't know what I am going to do!

RICH: And how are your other two children?

SANDY: They're starting to get upset also.

RICH: What happens next?

[*Sandy pauses for a few moments.*]

SANDY: [*softly*] I don't know.

[*There is a silence. I wait for a few moments to see if Sandy has more to say. But there continues to be dead silence. Instinctively, I decide to move on.*]

RICH: I am going to count from five to one and you are going to be at the next significant event in this life. Five, four, three, two, one: You are there. Tell me what you might have a glimpse of.

SANDY: I am indoors.

RICH: What are you doing?

[*Sandy tilts her head down, appearing very sad.*]

SANDY: I'm sitting on the couch.

RICH: What's happening?

[*In my office, tears fall from Sandy's eyes. She speaks slowly and softly.*]

SANDY: I'm crying. I have my head in my hands.

RICH: What happens next?

[*Sandy stops crying.*]

SANDY: I look up to see a man I know.

RICH: What does he look like?

SANDY: He is tall, thin; he has a beard.

RICH: Why is he there?

SANDY: He's explaining something to me.

RICH: What does he say?

SANDY: He tells me that my son is not coming home. That he seems to be lost. No one can find him and it has been a few days now.

RICH: How do you feel?

SANDY: *Very* upset!

[*Sandy begins to cry again.*]

RICH: Is there anyone else there?

SANDY: My fifteen-year-old is here.

RICH: What is he doing?

SANDY: He has his arm around me and he is trying to comfort me.

RICH: What happens next?

[*She pauses for a while.*]

SANDY: I don't know.

[*I think to myself that I do not know what to do with this, but I am sure that there is a bigger meaning in this than even I know. I don't know what connections to make. I don't know how to make something positive out of this. I have the sense that there is a greater power at work here, and I very much have faith that this power will bring something good to this session. I try to go with my own intuition in terms of what to do next. Then the thought comes to me that I want to take Sandy to the end of this lifetime.*]

RICH: Since you cannot seem to get much more from this moment in time, I want to take you to the *end* of this lifetime.

SANDY: Okay.

RICH: I am going to count back from five. Five, four, three, two, one: You are now at the end of this lifetime. Tell me when you get a glimpse of what is going on at this moment in time.

[*Sandy's voice is weak.*]

SANDY: I'm lying down. I am feeling sick and I am feeling sad.

RICH: How do you look?

SANDY: I have white hair.

RICH: Is there anyone there with you?

SANDY: Oh yes, my older son.

RICH: What is he doing?

SANDY: He's comforting me.

RICH: And what about your daughter?

SANDY: She's okay but she is not here.

RICH: What happens next?

[*Sandy pauses and doesn't seem to have much more to say. Once again, I think to myself, "Where do I want to go with this?" Feeling persistently optimistic that something good will come of this, I tell Sandy that I want to take her to the* very end *of this lifetime. Again I count down from five to one.*]

RICH: You are at the *very end* of this lifetime. What is happening?

[*Sandy's face begins to look peaceful.*]

SANDY: I am starting to feel very light.

RICH: Light?

SANDY: I am starting to feel like I am *floating*.

RICH: What else?

[*Sandy begins to smile.*]

SANDY: I am feeling *great*!

RICH: What year is it?

SANDY: 1836.

RICH: Continue to tell me how you are feeling.

SANDY: Now I am feeling very light and I am floating above my body.

RICH: Where are you floating?

SANDY: I am floating up toward the light.

RICH: Tell me more.

[*Sandy looks very excited and her smile is bigger than ever.*]

SANDY: I'm feeling *very* good. I'm feeling better than I have in my *whole life*!

RICH: And what happens next?

SANDY: I'm going further up toward the light.

RICH: And what else?

SANDY: I see my twelve-year-old son!

[*I get chills up my spine. The expression on Sandy's face is peaceful and gently smiling. There is a great sense of joy with being reunited with her twelve-year-old son. I give Sandy a few moments to enjoy this miraculous reunion.*]

RICH: And what happens next?

SANDY: Well, I'm looking down toward my body still, and I see my fifteen-year-old next to my body. But you know what?

RICH: What?

SANDY: My fifteen-year-old, my older son, was the stillborn son I had in this lifetime!

[*At this point, I have chills going up and down my whole body.*]

RICH: How does that feel?

SANDY: It feels great! I have never felt so great in my whole life.

[*I begin to see the bigger lesson here. The spirit has brought the lesson to both of us.*]

RICH: What is the significance of this?

SANDY: You *never* lose anyone you love! They're *always* with you!

[*I feel great joy and relief myself.*]

RICH: Is there anything else?

SANDY: No, I just feel very, very good. I can't even describe how *good* I feel! There are no words to describe how I feel right now.

[*I let Sandy enjoy that for a few moments.*]

RICH: Do you feel finished for now? [*I sense that she is.*]

SANDY: Yes.

RICH: You can stay where you are for a few more moments and when you're ready, you can let me know and I'll bring you back into this room.

[*Sandy pauses.*]

SANDY: I'm ready.

I then brought her back into the room. When we reviewed this experience, Sandy kept telling me that there were no words to describe what she had just experienced. There was so much relief, not only that she was rejoined with her twelve-year-old son, but also that she finally felt closure with the baby she had lost thirty years earlier. Sandy left the office with a great sense of peace and relief.

The following week, Sandy and I carefully reviewed the profound significance of her second past life regression experience.

"You know what, Rich?"

"What?"

"I thought about that experience all the way home. I went over and over it again for the next few days, and you know what I realized?"

"What?"

"Last week was the anniversary of my son's death!"

"Wow!" I responded. "That's amazing."

"And for the first time in all these years, I didn't feel the need to visit his grave. I think I finally feel at peace with it."

This experience was an adventure in soul travel and divine intervention for both of us. It resonated with Sandy on so many levels. It is a very spiritual experience, to know that you are always connected—either in the past, present, or future—to the people you love. The bigger picture gave Sandy a sense of comfort that, no matter what happens in this life, it's always temporary; you never really die or lose the people you love. You never need to fear that people you love will abandon you because the connections that love creates are eternal. With that, Sandy found a sense of peace that she never could have imagined before. She always thought of herself as a person with deep compassion and faith. By alleviating much of her fear of conflict and loss, Sandy attained the peace of mind that there is a lesson to be learned in all experiences, even those that are the most traumatic.

In regards to Sandy's husband Mark, he spent several months in the hospital and endured multiple surgeries to repair the damage caused by his burns. After he recovered enough to be released, we met regularly for therapy sessions over the next two years. He wanted very much to heal in all ways from his horrible ordeal. He has since succeeded in his recovery, and currently leads a calmer, meaningful, and more rewarding life.

My doctrine is:
Live so that thou mayest desire to live again
—that is thy duty—
for in any case thou wilt again
—Nietzsche (German philosopher; 1844–1900)

Chapter 12

Case Study D

Love's Bond Endures:
Encountering the Spirit Guide

The important thing is not to stop questioning. Curiosity has its own reason for existing. One cannot help but be in awe when he contemplates the mysteries of eternity, of life, of the marvelous structure of reality. It is enough if one tries merely to comprehend a little of this mystery every day. Never lose a holy curiosity.

—Albert Einstein

Sandy had a great past life regression experience. It helped her find peace in regard to most of her current life issues. But months later, Sandy had more questions about bigger issues in life. The bigger issues for Sandy were whether or not she was going in the right direction and what her life purpose was. In order to get some answers to these questions, Sandy told me that she really wanted to go deeper. Her fantasy was that I could somehow help her meet a spirit guide or guardian angel. I shared with Sandy that this wish was difficult to achieve, but at the same time I believed it to be quite possible. Coincidentally, I had recently returned from a retreat with a woman named Doreen Virtue, a popular psychologist and author who is best known for contacting her patients' angels and spirit guides.

I told Sandy, "If this is your wish, I will do everything I can to help facilitate this experience for you."

"I would love it," she replied.

"Once again, I can't guarantee anything will come of the effort. But I believe whatever *does* come of it will be an enjoyable experience."

"Whenever you're ready, I'm ready," replied Sandy.

I started her on a hypnotic induction that would help move her in a different direction:

RICH: In this wonderful state of peace and relaxation, you now find yourself in a beautiful garden. It is a place where there is no time or no space. It is a place of wisdom and love. You walk around this garden and you find a bench where you can sit and rest. While you are sitting and resting and feeling very peaceful, imagine that a wise and loving being comes to join you in this garden. And imagine that you can communicate with this being, whether through words or symbols or images, thoughts, or feelings. It doesn't matter how you communicate: You can communicate any way you need to. You can ask a question and listen for the answer. You can ask for what you need. This being could be a guide, a friend, a reflection of your higher self, or an angel; it's your choice. Ask for who you need. So take a moment and imagine this wise and loving being coming to join you. And as you do that, let me know if you have any sensation. It could be visual or any of your senses or feelings; it could also just be awareness. You can communicate with me and still remain in your deeply relaxed state.

[*Several moments pass. Sandy's eyes squint, as if she is trying to make an image come into focus.*]

SANDY: I keep seeing an old, old man.

[*I reinforce the visualization.*]

RICH: An old, old man.

SANDY: With a cane.

RICH: With a cane…

SANDY: And a long beard.

RICH: Okay.

[*Sandy's eyes probe up and down underneath her eyelids.*]

SANDY: And he has on, like, a robe, but it's not really a robe.

It's more like what a monk would wear, but white.

RICH: Okay.

SANDY: He's sitting.

RICH: Where?

SANDY: On the bench.

RICH: On the bench with you?

SANDY: Yeah.

[*Sandy's face appears serene.*]

RICH: And how are you feeling?

SANDY: Very peaceful.

RICH: Okay. And what happens next?

SANDY: I just sense myself getting *more* peaceful.

RICH: Enjoy that feeling. Take that energy in. Let this being's presence radiate into *your* presence. It's a communication that says, "I'm with you."

[*I pause for a moment. Sandy's body continues to move and her head sways slightly.*]

SANDY: I feel like he's trying to tell me something.

RICH: Listen closely. *Hear* what he's telling you.

[*Sandy appears like there's a whisper in her ear.*]

SANDY: He's telling me to come with him.

RICH: Do you want to go with him?

SANDY: Yeah.

RICH: So why don't you go with him and tell me where he takes you.

[*Moments pass as I perceive something happening to Sandy.*]

RICH: Where is he taking you?

SANDY: I don't *see* anything but I *feel*.

RICH: What are you feeling?

[*Sandy appears very serene once again.*]

SANDY: Peace.

[*I continue to press further.*]

RICH: Where do you feel he's taking you?

SANDY: I feel like he's taking me to meet somebody.

RICH: Okay, then go with him. Continue on your journey. Tell me his name.

SANDY: Now I see someone else who is all white.

[*I interpret instinctively.*]

RICH: This seems to be another guide. Can you ask him his name? What does he say?

SANDY: He says (his name is) Tom.

RICH: Tom? His name is Tom?

SANDY: Yeah, though he doesn't really say it.

[*I think to myself that "Tom" sounds like a nickname. Angels and spirit guides are usually identified by formal names. I question Sandy further.*]

RICH: Tom?

[*Sandy replies firmly.*]

SANDY: His name is *Tom*!

RICH: Okay. What do you want to ask Tom? Think of a question for Tom. Ask him any question you would like. What is that question?

SANDY: I want to ask him how many angels or spirit guides I have with me.

RICH: You can do that right now.

[*Sandy pauses to silently ask her question. She verbalizes the answer.*]

SANDY: Three.

RICH: Three?

SANDY: And Tom is one of them.

[*I am still skeptical about this "Tom" entity.*]

RICH: Tom. Is he an angel or is he a spirit guide?

[*Sandy is silent for a moment.*]

RICH: What does he say?

SANDY: He says *Gabrielle* is my spirit guide.

RICH: Gabrielle is your spirit guide?

SANDY: Yes.

[*I go back to Tom.*]

RICH: And who is Tom?

SANDY: He's my *friend.*

RICH: He's your friend. And who is the *third* one?

SANDY: The Angel of Peace.

RICH: Does the Angel of Peace have a name?

SANDY: He just wants to be called the Angel of Peace.

[*I decide not to argue.*]

RICH: Okay.

SANDY: And Tom wants me to know that I am always protected. And *he's* the protector.

[*I can't let this Tom thing go.*]

RICH: Does Tom have *another* name? Does he have another name that we all know him by? Tom seems like a nickname.

SANDY: He's not answering.

[*I give up.*]

RICH: Okay, so you have three angels and spirit guides. You have Tom, you have Gabrielle, and you have the Angel of Peace.

SANDY: Yeah. Tom says that he is in front of me and the other two are beside me.

RICH: Has Tom ever lived on this earth?

SANDY: Yes.

RICH: Okay. Has he lived here at the same time you have or before…

[*Sandy interrupts me in mid-sentence.*]

SANDY: Oh my God!

[*Sandy is shocked.*]

RICH: What is that?

[*I try to imagine what Sandy is experiencing.*]

SANDYS: I think it's my son, the one who died before birth!

[*Chills go up my spine.*]

RICH: Okay. It's okay.

[*I try to reassure Sandy that her shocking realization is okay.*]

SANDY: Oh my God!

[*Sandy's body is trembling. Again I try to reassure her.*]

RICH: It's okay. You're safe and it's okay. This is where it all comes together! You have known your son in the past and you will know your son in the future. You have souls that surround you that travel with you from lifetime to lifetime. Sometimes they live with you in the same lifetime and sometimes they will wait for you on the other side.

[*Sandy's panic subsides as it all starts to make sense. She takes a slow, deep breath. Serenity flows all over her body. She begins to talk calmly and softly.*]

SANDY: He's waiting for me on the other side!

RICH: You are always connected because love always lasts. Love is eternal and that's why it is a comforting feeling, because you never lose anyone. You are always connected to anyone that you love, here on Earth *and* on the other side. So you never really *lost* your son. He's there for you always! Love never ends. Love is eternal. Tom is *always* there with you.

SANDY: [*crying*] That was what we were going to name him!

RICH: That's why he is so important. And now he is there to be your *protector*. He's there to give you comfort. He's there guiding you and he's connected with you just as much as if he were here.

SANDY: And that's why he gave me the other two. He *picked* the other two.

RICH: He picked the other two?

SANDY: Yeah. And that's why one is the Angel of Peace.

RICH: Because?

SANDY: He wants me to have *peace.*

RICH: He wants you to always have peace.

SANDY: That's why there is no other name.

RICH: Well, that makes perfect sense now. That makes perfect sense.

[*Sandy looks very peaceful. Then suddenly her face lights up with excitement.*]

SANDY: He says that he is going to see me again!

RICH: *When* will he see you again?

SANDY: In *this* lifetime.

RICH: In this lifetime? Hmm, *when* will that happen?

SANDY: He can't tell me that!

[*Sandy pauses once again.*]

SANDY: He wants me to let the sadness go.

RICH: Are you able to let the sadness go?

[*Sandy speaks softly.*]

SANDY: I don't know.

RICH: What sadness is left?

SANDY: I guess for what *could* have been.

RICH: The way things could have been?

SANDY: But it's okay. He's telling me it's okay.

[*Sandy appears peaceful once again.*]

RICH: There's a good reason for things being the way they've been. Do you know that?

SANDY: He's saying it was a lesson.

RICH: And what's the lesson?

SANDY: Life.

RICH: What's the lesson about life?

SANDY: It goes on.

RICH: Life always goes on.

SANDY: And that's a good thing.

RICH: And there's never really a loss.

SANDY: No.

RICH: No one ever dies. You never lose anyone.

[*Sandy pauses again to reflect.*]

RICH: That's the lesson you're learning.

SANDY: That's my purpose.

RICH: And your purpose is what?

SANDY: To understand that life never ends.

RICH: Beautiful.

SANDY: And it continues.

RICH: Okay. And what should be your direction in this life?

SANDY: To help people. And to help people love one another.

RICH: Hmm. You do that well.

SANDY: That's what he says!

[*We both laugh.*]

RICH: So your purpose is to help build the love in this world. And to help others learn the same lessons.

SANDY: He's telling me that he's always going to be with me. And that he's okay, and that he's with God. And what could be better than that?

RICH: Right.

[*Sandy pauses and listens for a moment.*]

SANDY: It's time to go. He's telling me.

RICH: He's telling you it's time. Okay. How are you feeling?

SANDY: He says there is going to be peace in my life now.

RICH: That's reassuring. And you're on that road to peace. You've learned many lessons already.

SANDY: I keep seeing my parents.

RICH: You keep seeing your parents?

SANDY: Yeah.

RICH: What about them?

SANDY: I think they are going to be with Tom soon. And he says that's okay.

RICH: Because if that's true, you still don't lose them.

SANDY: I think that's what he's trying to tell me.

RICH: So if something happens soon, you don't need to be so sad.

SANDY: That's right.

RICH: So it's important *you* know that also.

SANDY: I know that now.

RICH: How do you feel now?

[*Sandy takes a deep breath and exclaims loud and clear.*]

SANDY: Happy!

RICH: Happy! Are you ready to start coming back?

SANDY: Yeah.

RICH: Okay. Hold on to the happy feeling because happy is

what your angels and guides *want* you to feel: happiness and love and peace, all around you, all the time. Happiness and love and peace: connectedness. They are all eternal; they all surround you. You just have to see it for yourself. So enjoy that, *bathe* in that. There's no need to fear because you are always protected. You are always connected. So enjoy that sense of love and peace and happiness. And keep in mind that you will remember all of this when you come back into this room. You will remember all of this that you have learned, all of this insight, all of this that gives you comfort and peace.

Sandy came back feeling completely refreshed and rejuvenated.

"Oh my God! That was really unbelievable! That was a real answer to my prayers," she said.

As a result of her experience in this last regression, Sandy discovered that the people she loves remain with her always, despite even death. The sense of longing and loss she experienced at their passing has been replaced by a feeling of deep connection and enduring love. The realization that they are with her as guides and protectors has given her a newfound sense of peace, contentment, and well-being which she continues to carry with her.

There is no death, only a change of worlds.
—Duwamish Tribe Chief Seattle (c. 1784-1866)

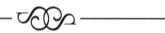

༄༅ **Chapter 13** ༄༅

Sometimes the Good Die Young for a Reason

*Life is the coexistence of all opposite values. Joy and sorrow,
pleasure and pain... birth and death. All experience is by contrast,
and one would be meaningless without the other.*

—Deepak Chopra

M y first personal experience with the death of someone close to me occurred when I was nineteen and away at college. About a week before Christmas, I got a phone call from home. It was my older brother's wife, Jeannie. I was surprised to hear from her since I never heard from her or my brother Gerry while I was away at school. In fact, I never heard from anyone in my family until I went home on a weekend every now and then. It wasn't that no one cared; it was just that we weren't great communicators.

As the third child of five, I was the quietest member of my family. From a safe and silent distance I waited to see if my parents were speaking to each other, if my father was in a bad mood after work, or if my youngest brother had misbehaved in school again and was about to get a beating. My mind analyzed all the conversations that led to the conflicts and violence; I did what I could whenever possible to avoid it.

But I learned early on that the best way of staying out of trouble in my family was to keep my mouth closed and my eyes open. I became neutral territory in the war zone that was my family. Most of the time, the dialogue remained in my head, except for those occasions when my father lamented to me about my brother, or my mother complained to me about my father. None of them seemed able to talk to each other, but they all talked to me. And as I listened,

134

my mind clung desperately to a private fantasy of how a family should be.

When her first husband, William Harrell, died as the result of injuries sustained in WWII, my mother found herself alone, a widow with two small children, Gerry and Lynne. In 1952 she met and married Irving Scheinberg, and I was born the following year. My brother, Mark, arrived in 1956, and the youngest, Scott, three years later. My father worked fifty to sixty hours per week to make sure he could pay the bills and put food on the table. Unquestionably, my father worked very hard but was often weary and angry with my mother. He would lash out violently if she tried to speak up and challenge him.

In the midst of this turmoil, we kids found ways to cope with the situation. Mark insulated himself from the emotional chaos by surrounding himself with friends at all times; in fact, today Mark recalls a much happier childhood than I do. My parents loved having his friends at the house, and indulged them with snacks. Their presence seemed always to diffuse any tension in the air. Mark helped my parents demonstrate a loving intent with this constant entourage.

My sister Lynne, eight years my senior, became like a mother to me, waking me in the morning and helping me get ready for school. Smart, strong-willed and defiant, she graduated from high school early, and at the age of sixteen left home to go to nursing school. A year later, in a fit of rage brought on by a disagreement about money, my father essentially kicked Lynne out of the family and we were all forbidden to have any contact with her. Of course, at first we found ways to circumvent my father's orders. My brother Gerry, who had recently gotten married, had his own house, and we would arrange to meet secretly with Lynne there. Eventually, I went off to college. Only Scott, the youngest, remained vulnerable. He was very bright but was diagnosed as hyperactive; frequent complaints from school exacerbated family tensions. Such was the emotional rollercoaster that we called home.

The world outside my house presented a similar dichotomy. Every night on the news, I watched soldiers dying and children being burned by napalm in the name of freedom and democracy. I watched the hippies preaching, "Make love, not war," as they staged angry protests and took over college campuses. Powerful voices for peace and justice, Robert Kennedy and Martin Luther King, Jr. were both silenced by gunmen's bullets. My counterculture heroes, Jimi Hendrix, Jim Morrison, and Janis Joplin, each of them eventually fell victim to their own excesses. At nineteen, I worried what I would do if I were drafted, and the only real peace I had was the one which I preserved, silently, in my head.

Our clandestine relationship with Lynne continued sporadically for almost nine years. Then, in the summer of 1972, at the age of twenty-six, Lynne appeared unannounced at a family barbeque. We all held our collective breath as she came face to face with my father for the first time in nearly a decade. To my amazement, nothing was said about the past by Lynne or my father. It was as if it had never happened and the gathering continued without incident. As abruptly as she had been ousted, Lynne was back in the family. And seeing that the violent family dynamic had now become focused on a very troubled eleven-year-old Scott, she offered to take him to live with her in Florida. He moved there with her that September.

During Christmas break that year, one morning Jeannie called me and said, "You need to come home."

"Why?" I asked. "What's the matter?"

"Someone's sick," Jeannie replied mechanically.

At this point, I knew something terrible had happened. My family never made an issue about anyone just being sick. "Who's sick?" I asked.

"We'll talk about it when you come home. Your mother needs you."

That confirmed it. I knew someone had died. That would be the only reason my mother needed me. I knew not to ask any more questions and just come home.

I had asked Lynne, when we had a few moments alone the summer she came back, what exactly had happened between her and my father all those years ago. She confirmed the violence and abuse I had long suspected but then added quickly, "I didn't come back to cause any more problems. I don't want what I said today to cause a problem between you and Dad. That was the past and there's no sense talking about it anymore."

In spite of the time we were apart, the love between Lynne and I never wavered. We always had a special bond, though we didn't talk for long stretches of time. I respected her wish not to answer any more questions. Though she never finished nursing school, she had always been a compassionate and selfless caregiver. At home in Florida, Lynne was not only taking care of Scott, but she had also befriended a coworker who was going through a difficult divorce. Lynne let Nancy and her three young children share her tiny one-bedroom apartment for two months while Nancy pursued legal action against her often violent and abusive husband.

After Jeannie's call, I arrived home to find my family in shambles. Scott had just flown in from Florida for the Christmas break. Lynne, having only a few days off for the holiday, was supposed to join us on Christmas Eve. But now she would not be joining us, not for Christmas, not ever. Lynne had been killed. Senseless brutality and rage had stolen my sister from me; violence had torn my family apart once again; and once again I found myself haunted by the angry and empty feeling that I had struggled with since childhood. This was the sense that God had never been a part of my life.

I learned that Lynne had agreed to accompany Nancy when she picked up her children after a weekend visitation with their father, hoping to avoid any dangerous outbursts. Once they pulled into the driveway, Nancy went into the trailer to pick up her children while Lynne waited in the car. When Nancy stepped inside, she was immediately confronted by Robert, her soon-to-be ex-husband, who had apparently been drinking all day. An altercation followed and Robert took out his gun and shot her. Robert stormed outside to the car where my sister Lynne sat in terror. He fired a shot at her through the car window, the bullet penetrating her hand as she raised it in an attempt to shield herself. With her hand bloodied, Robert ordered her into the house where his wife lay wounded. Once inside, he shot them both again. Nancy survived, even after the fourth bullet. But the second shot he aimed at my sister entered her heart and killed her.

The days that followed were torturous. During the wake there was a lot of chatter in my head, but I said or felt very little. I was completely numb. I was traumatized. I never cried. Not even when I stared in Lynne's face in that open casket. Not even when it was obvious that makeup could not conceal her injured, folded hands. And I knew her pretty dress did little to conceal the knowledge that there was a hole in her chest. This was my Christmas, 1972.

I returned to college in January. The surreal numbness permeated my very soul. I had a very hard time sleeping. My inner turmoil could not be censored once the lights went out and I struggled night after sleepless night. What little sleep I managed to get was disrupted by confused and frightening dreams.

One such nightmare woke me abruptly in the early morning hours. My father and I were together, holding a gun. Then we both placed the gun into my sister's mouth and pulled the trigger. I woke up frantically. How could this be? My logical mind could not understand how I could have had anything to do with Lynne's death. After all, I always kept to myself. I always kept out of harm's way. But I couldn't escape my emotional self. Deep inside, I felt guilty for doing nothing. I did not love my sister in the way she needed to be loved. I wasn't available to her for many years. I didn't protect or defend her. I didn't take any risks, as she would have. I was no better to her than my father. I did not challenge him when he locked her out of our lives. My silence had made me a co-conspirator.

I couldn't sleep for two weeks. There was no peace in my head.

I was alone, at college, suffering in silence, wishing for peace. In my dorm room one afternoon, I was feeling very sad and solitary. I laid my head down and drifted off to sleep. Then I had a dream. I was home, on Long Island, in the yard. The sun was shining. There was a gentle breeze. Then I saw my sister, Lynne. She appeared to be drifting down from the sky. I watched as she came closer. She stopped directly in front of me. I knew that she was *very* real. She was smiling; she was happy and peaceful. Then she touched me, and I instantly felt peaceful too. A warm, quiet comfort spread throughout my body. Then she gently, gradually moved away, back toward the sky, and disappeared.

Suddenly, I woke up. Contrary to the way I was feeling just before my afternoon nap, I was now feeling completely at *peace*. I knew that Lynne had come to ease my pain. There was no more guilt and no more internal chatter, only a warm feeling in my mind and my body that she was okay. *Everything* was okay. The love between us was still strong. The love never died.

Lynne did not contact me again until years later.

I had finished my degree in psychology and returned to school to complete my master's degree in social work. I found myself loving the work of helping people work out a myriad of life's challenges, most of which I had experienced firsthand in my own life. My desire was to somehow know, feel, and appreciate all life experiences. Spiritually, I always longed to know the bigger, deeper meaning of all things having to do with the life force itself.

By the '90s, I felt that my life's purpose and direction was pretty clear. I was happy and successful in my life and my career, and I began to reflect on my first forty-five years. As I did so, my thoughts returned to my sister Lynne. What was her purpose in life? Why did fate only give her twenty-six years? I started to think about her a lot.

Soon, it became clear to me that I was not only thinking about Lynne; I was *feeling* her. I was experiencing a persistent sense that she was with me spiritually. I didn't question it. In fact, it was comforting to feel her presence around me so often. It reminded me of the way she had taken care of me when I was a child, the way she had made me feel cared for and loved.

I felt as if I were being directed somehow when I came across a catalog of courses being held in upstate New York at a retreat center. For the first time I considered spending a whole weekend at a conference that was a long way from home.

"A Conference on Soul Survival: Exploring the Evidence of Life After Death," was a topic I could not resist looking into. The conference featured Brian Weiss, MD; Raymond Moody, MD, PhD; David Morehouse, PhD; and Char Margolis, an internationally known psychic intuitive. Little did I know that my sister was leading me to one of the great turning points of my life.

Raymond Moody, best known for his book *Life After Life (2001)*, presented a riveting lecture about near-death experiences and the efforts that have been made throughout history to contact loved ones after death. The concepts he spoke of were not new to me, but his lecture brought into focus their application in my work. I found myself fascinated and intrigued by the incredible healing that could be made possible by such communication.

Likewise, the lecture given by David Morehouse was of particular interest to me. His book, *Psychic Warrior (1998)*, is a compelling account of his spiritual awakening after the US military trained him for the Stargate Project, a top-secret group of psychic spies backed by the CIA and the Defense Intelligence Agency. After his military service, Morehouse was convinced that he must use the knowledge he obtained to further the cause of peace. He is currently a popular lecturer and trainer.

Meeting Brian Weiss provided my first formal introduction to the science and practice of hypnosis and past life regression. He was a great speaker and I found his demeanor very humble, gentle, and warmly engaging. Though I did not realize it fully at the time, his presentation on past life regression would have a profound and lasting impact on my life.

But as I attended this remarkable and stimulating conference, in fact it was actually the psychic Char Margolis whom I was most anxious to see.

Char presented a description and summary of her experiences as a psychic to an audience of over two hundred people. I was determined to be one of the five individuals that were called up to the stage for an individual reading. I was hungry for some validation of my sense that Lynne's spirit had indeed been connecting with me for the preceding two years.

When I was actually called to come forward, I was not really surprised. The overwhelming desire to be "read" by this phenomenal psychic seemed almost predestined. Admittedly, I was very nervous about being on a stage in front of a large crowd, but I was determined to stay focused on what had become a personal mission to confirm Lynne's spiritual presence in my life.

"You have a few people around you that have passed," Char began.

"Yes," I replied solemnly.

"Let me see if I can get a name," Char added. She paused.

"I'm getting a *b...r...t...a*," Char continued, trying to put these random letters together.

Char looked upward, then back at me, then upward again. "Bertha?" she blurted out, then paused again. "No, Berta? Does Berta mean anything to you?"

Shivers ran up my spine. "Berta was my great-grandmother," I replied as I started to shake.

I thought, "This is the woman who lived with us on and off throughout my childhood." My mother always told me that my great-grandmother secretly had a special place in her heart for me because I had been born with a cleft palate. Granny Berta had given birth to her own child with a cleft palate many years earlier, but that child had starved to death. There was no way to surgically repair the birth defect at the time, and therefore the baby could not swallow properly.

"Berta wants you to know that she is right here and she is looking after you," continued Char.

I continued to sit speechlessly in amazement up on the stage.

"You have a young woman in your life that has passed?" asked Char.

"Yes, my sister," I replied.

"Well she is here too," commented Char.

I was not convinced that this was true. I looked up at Char suspiciously.

"Let's see if I can get another name," Char persisted. "I'm getting an *l...n...e*. Lenny? No, there's a *y*. Lynn?" asked Char.

I was dumbfounded. "Her name was Lynne," I replied. "L-y-n-n-e."

"Lynne seems to be one of the main people who are looking after you from the other side. She is one of your guides and she wants you to know that she is always with you."

I started to sob while sitting in my chair on stage, unable to speak and oblivious to the two hundred people in the audience who watched quietly in anticipation of what might happen next.

"Lynne says that she is worried about Mary. Who is Mary?" asked Char.

"My mother," I blurted out.

"Lynne says that she wishes that she was here to help you with your mother. Is she sick?"

"Yes, she has emphysema. She's on oxygen," I replied very softly, with tears still streaming down my cheeks.

"There seems to be one more, a young male energy. Is this someone you know?" asked Char.

"Yes, my brother."

"You have *two* siblings that have died?" Char asked, seeming a little surprised.

"Yes."

Once again, Char looked up briefly to find a name. "It's a *g* name," she declared. "Gerard. No, Gerald," she declared.

"Yes Gerald," I replied. Char was unbelievably accurate. My older brother Gerry had died of cirrhosis of the liver in 1997.

"Well let's see if your brother and sister have a message for you," Char stated. Then she paused for a few moments.

"I'm seeing a ball, a beach ball. Does that mean anything?"

"Well, when I grew up, we lived by the beach on Long Island."

"Is there anything special about a beach ball?" prompted Char.

"I'm not sure," I replied. "I mean, we probably used to play with a beach ball together at the beach when I was younger, but I don't remember a specific time."

"Well, they're telling me that they really enjoyed tossing the beach ball around with you."

"Okay," I replied softly, now emotionally exhausted from the reading.

"Well, they all want you to know that they're here with you now and they'll all be part of the welcoming committee years from now when it's your turn to cross over." Then Char concluded her reading. My head was spinning, but I managed to descend slowly and safely from the stage. When I returned to my seat, I quickly jotted down notes about the whole experience, making sure that I would not forget any detail. As I wrote, I was still somewhat puzzled about the exact reference to the beach ball story.

All four presenters made for an eye-opening, consciousness-raising weekend. But Char's reading felt like a spiritual awakening and an affirmation of many of the psychic moments I had been experiencing for several years prior.

When I got home, I couldn't wait to tell my wife all about the experience. Eventually I got to the part of the weekend where I began to describe the great reading I had received. I pulled out my page of notes and I proceeded to describe every delicious detail. Then I got to the end of the story when Char said, "Your brother and sister want you to know that they really enjoyed tossing the beach ball around with you."

"Oh my God!" screamed Geraldine.

"What?" I said, puzzled by her reaction.

"Don't you remember?" she asked.

"Remember? Remember what?" I asked.

"Don't you remember tossing the beach ball around with your brother and sister? We were all at Anna's house together. The three of you were in the backyard, in her pool. It was the last time the three of you were together. It was during the summer when you were home from college and Lynne reconciled with your father. It was the last summer we were all together before you went back to school and she died."

My body started shaking all over. "You're right," I exclaimed. "I can't believe you remembered! Now I remember."

Just like every other person's life in this book, my life has been a series of hardships and blessings throughout the journey. In my own life, there are many challenges I have come to recognize as turning points during my childhood, adolescence, and adult years.

It is only through hard times that I have been prompted to do the deepest soul-searching. After all, when you're coasting through life, you don't take the time to value or reassess it. It is only through adversity that I have been able to grow emotionally, evolve spiritually, and discover the direction and meaning of my whole life.

When I was nineteen years old and I found out that my sister had been murdered, I went into emotional shock. I could not think. I could not feel. Nothing in this world made any sense to me. After all, if there was a God and He had a plan, how could He let this tragedy happen? How could my poor sister, in her attempt to help a friend and her children escape a violent environment, be rewarded with being brutally shot to death?

Now that it is many, many years later, I know that it *all* makes sense. I believe now that my sister actually *planned* to come into this world for only twenty-six years, *before she was born*. Her purpose in this lifetime was to teach the rest of our family, her *soul mates*, some very important lessons about life and love. She taught my father that being angry and hurtful never gets your point across. He became a much calmer and more supportive father and grandfather after her death. Lynne taught my mother to be more demonstrative and loving, even when it felt risky and left her open to disappointment and hurt. Lynne's death forced each of us to reconsider ourselves, our behaviors, our directions.

Lynne's death also taught me many lessons about how to live and live fully. Among those lessons, I have learned to never miss the chance to tell others that I love them because I know that I may not get another chance to do so. I also now know that death never ends a relationship; love is just shared from the heart on a new, deeper level. Lynne is *not* dead to me. I know now that she is just with me in a new form: as my spirit guide. I am now sure that my sister died for a reason, that both her life and death was part of a much larger plan: a divine plan.

Lynne's spirit continues to guide me in my day-to-day life. Most of each day, I can be very busy going places, doing things and just generally carrying on with the mechanical business of life. But at night, before I go to sleep, I have the chance to transcend *deeper*. I get a chance to think about how many lives I have touched and how many others have touched me. I stop and appreciate the many blessings of everyone I have met in this life, as well as the soul mates, spirit guides, and past lives that have been very much a part of me.

I have come to appreciate that my spiritual revelations have helped me to gain deep understanding about my past. I have been able to forgive and to heal. It is now my personal passion to pass onto others the blessings I have already received. So late at night, when the air is still, I feel much more peaceful than in my younger days. Now there is insight. Now there is hope. I no longer feel alone. I now realize we are *all* connected. Love is the nature of that connection. It is boundless and everlasting. This awareness now eases me into my sleep and my dreams.

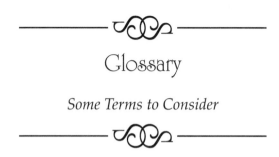

Glossary

Some Terms to Consider

After Death Communication (ADC): The manifestation, sign or other communication from a deceased person to one who is living. This communication can be received directly or through a medium, who acts as a conduit for the communication.

Angels: A spiritual entity found in many religions. Angels are usually viewed as emanations of a supreme divine being, sent to do the tasks of that being. Although the nature of angels and the tasks given to them vary from tradition to tradition, in Christianity, Judaism, and Islam, they often act as messengers from God. Other roles in religious traditions include acting as warrior or guard; the concept of a guardian angel is popular in modern Western culture.

Archetypal Roles: In the stories of our lives, we often find ourselves in roles we didn't even realize we chose to play. Psychologist Carl Jung, one of the great minds of the modern era, called these roles and characters *archetypes*. He proposed that people go through life drawing from a repertoire of instinctive roles: father, mother, child, lover, creator, warrior, caregiver, and an untold number of others. Jung claimed there are as many archetypes "as there are typical situations in life."

Ascended Masters: Enlightened spiritual beings who once lived on Earth just like we do. Over the course of many lifetimes of devotion and striving, they fulfilled their mission and reason for being—their divine plan—and ascended back to their divine source, reuniting with Spirit.

Association: Psychological term referring to an emotional connection which is based on feeling or memories of similar experiences or individuals.

Carl Gustav Jung: (July 26, 1875 – June 6, 1961) was a Swiss psychiatrist, an influential thinker and the founder of analytical psychology. Jung's approach to psychology has been influential in the field of depth psychology and in countercultural movements across the globe. Jung is considered to be the first modern psychologist to state that human psyche is "by nature religious" and to explore it in depth.

Christ Consciousness: "Empty thyself and I shall fill thee." represents a single sentence message of Jesus Christ. In Christ Consciousness the focus is placed on the concept of Christ rather than the personality of Christ. This concept asserts that the Spirit is a *present* and not an event, content, or a creature in the passage of time which is usually dissected into the past, present and future. The Spirit has no past, no present, and no future.

Codependence: A psychological term referring to behavior wherein an individual exhibits too much, and often inappropriate, caring for persons who depend on him or her. A codependent is one side of a relationship between mutually needy people. The dependent, or obviously needy party(s), may have emotional, physical, financial difficulties or addictions they seemingly are unable to surmount. The "codependent" party exhibits behavior which controls, makes excuses for, pities, and takes other actions to perpetuate the obviously needy party's condition, because of their desire to be needed and fear of doing anything that would change the relationship.

Depression: A mental disorder characterized by a pervasive low mood, low self-esteem, and loss of interest or pleasure in normally enjoyable activities.

Divine Force: The transcendent force(s) or power(s) credited to divinities. The operation of transcendent power implies some form of divine intervention.

Dream Incubation: The ritual of going to sleep in a sacred place in anticipation of receiving a helpful dream from a divine benefactor. In this ritual, specific questions are framed and the dreamer focuses on his or her intent to receive answers or information leading to answers within the context of the dream.

Dysfunctional: The general condition of abnormal or unhealthy interpersonal behavior or interaction within a group.

Earth Plane: Our three dimensional world and our physical existence on Earth as seen within the confines of a three dimensional perspective.

Facilitator: Neutral member of a group who helps a group work together more effectively. Facilitators are process leaders only—they have no decision-making authority, nor do they contribute to the substance of the discussion. The facilitator's job is to lead the group process, help improve the group's communication, help them examine and solve problems, and aid them in making decisions.

Group Therapy: A form of psychotherapy in which one or more therapists treat a small group of clients together as a group. The interaction between group members provides an integral part of the therapy process by providing feedback and alternative perspectives within the group.

Higher Self: Based on the concept that each individual (re) incarnates into bodily form from its authentic energy source, or higher self, being sent to gain experience on the earth plane. When an individual dies, the energy stream from the higher self is withdrawn from the physical body. The higher self is always connected to each individual incarnation and guides the individual throughout their life. Once the individual life experience is completed, the life energy is drawn back to the higher self. All higher selves are one, being part of universal consciousness.

Hypervigilance: An enhanced state of sensory sensitivity accompanied by an exaggerated intensity of behaviors geared toward detecting threats. Hypervigilance is also accompanied by a state of increased anxiety which can cause exhaustion.

Hypnagogia: A term which refers to the transitional state between wakefulness and sleep. Transition to and from sleep may be accompanied by a wide variety of sensory experiences. These can occur in any modality, individually or combined, and range from the vague and barely perceptible to vivid hallucinations.

Interior Castle: St. Teresa of Avila envisioned the soul as "a castle made of a single diamond...in which there are many rooms, just as in Heaven there are many mansions." The term refers to the deepest part of one's soul. For a modern interpretation of St. Teresa's concept and meditations, refer to *Entering the Castle* by Carolyn Myss (2007).

Kabbalism: A body of mystical teachings of rabbinical origin, often based on an esoteric interpretation of the Hebrew Scriptures. Kabalah refers to a set of esoteric beliefs and practices that supplement traditional Jewish interpretations of the Bible and religious observances.

Karma: The philosophical explanation of karma can differ slightly between traditions, but the general concept is basically the same. Through the law of karma, the effects of all deeds actively create past, present, and future experiences, thus making one responsible for one's own life and the pain and joy it brings to him/her and others.

Law of Attraction: The principle that asserts that a person's thoughts (both conscious and unconscious) dictate the reality of their lives, whether or not they're aware of it.

Life Energy or Life Force: A term describing the concept of spiritual energy. Energy in this context is conceived of as a universal life force, the infinite and eternal source of all that exits.

Life Script: A term referring to a specific life environment we chose before being born. This includes the selection of our parents, siblings, and other people we will encounter, as well as the challenges and lessons to be learned in a particular life experience.

Lucid Dreaming: A dream in which the person is aware that they are dreaming while the dream is in progress, also known as a conscious dream. The dreamer can actively participate in and often manipulate the imaginary experiences in the dream environment. Lucid dreams can be extremely real and vivid depending on a person's level of self-awareness during the lucid dream.

Mediumship: The ability of a person (the medium) to experience contact with spirits of the dead, spirits of immaterial entities, angels, or demons. The medium generally attempts to facilitate communication between non-mediumistic people and spirits that have messages to share.

Metaphysics: A term used to describe the principles of reality transcending those of any particular science. It is concerned with explaining the ultimate nature of being and the world.

Mirror Gazing: A method of meditation in which the subject gazes into his or her own eyes in a mirror until the alternate images of self become visible. Often used as a vehicle for deeper self- awareness and accessing the subconscious self or as a means to communicate with spirits of the dead. (*See Psychomanteum*)

New American Bible: First published in 1970, an English Bible translation that was produced by members of the Catholic biblical scholars in cooperation with the United States Conference of Catholic Bishops.

Om: A mystical or sacred syllable in the Hindu, Jain, and Buddist religions. Commonly used as a mantra or chant during meditation, it is also believed that after a very long time of meditation the Purusha Sukta revealed the word Om (Aum) as being the truth.

Past lives: The collection of memories and emotions from a prior life experience, which are sometimes recalled spontaneously but which can also be accessed deliberately through hypnosis.

Past Life Regression Therapy: The exploration of past lives under guided self-hypnosis, for the purpose of discovering the experience's relationship to current distresses and healing them.

Psychomanteum: The psychomanteum is an ancient form of mirror gazing that has been popularized by Dr. Raymond Moody, MD, PhD. It has its roots in the oracles of ancient Greece. This type of mirror-gazing is used to contact spirits of departed loved ones.

Relaxation Response: Method of inducing a meditative state by a progressive relaxation of the body, beginning with the head and ending with the toes. The conscious focus on each body part induces a deep meditative state. The technique was originally developed by Herbert Benson, MD, and detailed in his book *The Relaxation Response*, published in 1975.

Soul: The non-physical part of a person, it is believed to consist of one's thoughts and personality, and can be synonymous with the spirit, mind or self. In theology, the soul is often believed to live on after the person's death, and some religions posit that God creates souls. In some cultures, nonhuman living things and sometimes inanimate objects are said to have souls, a belief known as animism.

Soul Mate: A term sometimes used to designate someone with whom one has an immediate feeling of deep and natural affinity, love, intimacy, sexuality, spirituality, and/or compatibility. It can also refer to the concept that souls are destined to encounter each other in one or more lifetimes for the purpose of learning or teaching a lesson in the pursuit of spiritual evolution.

Spirit Guide: A term used by the Western tradition of Spiritualist Churches, mediums, and psychics to describe an entity that remains a disincarnate spirit in order to act as a spiritual counselor or protector to a living incarnated human being.

Tantric: Referring to a religious philosophy according to which Shakti is usually the main deity worshipped, and the universe is regarded as the divine play of Shakti (the primordial cosmic energy) and Shiva (the supreme God). The philosophy deals primarily with spiritual practices and ritual forms of worship, which strive for rebirth and liberation from ignorance.

The Golden Rule: The philosophy of "Do unto others as you would have them do unto you."

Transcendental Meditation: A form of Eastern meditation that induces the subject to transcend the physical earthly plane through relaxation and introspection in a focused meditation practice. The technique was introduced to the Western world by the Maharishi

Mahesh Yogi from India in the late 1960s.

Transference: The redirection of feelings for one person to another, usually because of a psychological association. (*See association*)

Universal Consciousness: The collective wisdom, understanding, and energy that constitutes all consciousness.

Universal Oneness: the connectedness of all things as one in the energy that comprises them.

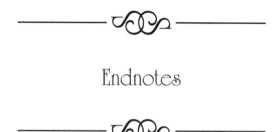

Endnotes

CHAPTER 1

1.   Anthony, E. James, M.D., Cohler, Bertram J., PhD. *The Invulnerable Child*, (New York: The Guilford Press, 1987).

2.   Goleman, Daniel. *Marriage: Research Reveals Ingredients of Happiness*, (*New York Times*, April 16, 1985).

CHAPTER 2

1.   *New Oxford American Dictionary*, 2nd ed., (Oxford University Press, 2005).

CHAPTER 4

1.   The original landmark research on the physiological correlates of the Transcendental Meditation technique was published in *Science, American Journal of Physiology*, and *Scientific American* in 1970-1972 (papers 1, 3, and 4). This research found that the Transcendental Meditation technique produces a physiological state of restful alertness. During the technique the physiology becomes deeply rested, as indicated by significant reductions in respiration, minute ventilation, tidal volume, and blood lactate, and significant increases in basal skin resistance (an index of relaxation). At the same time the physiology is alert rather than asleep, as indicated by an increased abundance of alpha waves in the EEG. These findings led researcher Dr. Keith Wallace to conclude that restful alertness is a fourth major state of consciousness, termed transcendental consciousness, which is physiologically distinct from ordinary waking, dreaming, and deep sleep (paper 2).

CHAPTER 6

1.   Schwartz, Gary E. and Simon, William, *The Afterlife Experiments*, (Atria Pub., 2003)

2.   Moody, Raymond, *Reunions*, (New York: Ivy Books, 1993) viii.

CHAPTER 7

1.   Aristotle, De Sommis, Trans. by Beare, J. and Ross, G. In Ross, W. (ed.) *The Works of Aristotle* (vol. 3) (London: Oxford University Press, 1931) as quoted in *Hypnagogia: The Unique State of Consciousness Between Wakefulness and Sleep* by Andreas Mavromatis (1987), 3.

2.   Bernd, E. Jr., *Relax* (Orlando, Florida: Greun Madainn Foundation, 1978) 28-9, as quoted in *Hypnagogia: The Unique State of Consciousness Between Wakefulness and Sleep* by Andreas Mavromatis (1987), 186.

CHAPTER 9

1.   Goldberg, Bruce, *"New Age Hypnosis,"* (St. Paul: Llewellyn Publications, 2001), 3.

2.   Ibid, 3.

3.   Stam, H.J. and Spanos, N.P. (1982*). The Asclepian Dream Healings and Hypnosis: A Critique. International Journal of Clinical and Experimental Hypnosis* 30(1): 9-22.

4.   Schneck, J.M. (1985). A history of the founding of the American Board of Medical Hypnosis. *American Journal of Clinical Hypnosis* 27(4): 241-244.

5.   There has been much research demonstrating the value of using hypnosis to assist with smoking cessation and weight loss. The following (6) studies document the correlation:

Crasilneck, Harold B. Ph.D. 1; Hall, James A. M.D. 2, The Use of Hypnosis in Controlling Cigarette Smoking. *Southern Medical Journal*.61(9):999-1002, September 1968.

Kline, Milton V. The use of extended group hypnotherapy sessions in controlling cigarette habituation. *International Journal of Clinical and Experimental Hypnosis*, Volume 18, Issue 4 October 1970, 270–282.

CHAPTER 9 continued

Stanton, H. E. A One-Session Hypnotic Approach to Modifying Smoking Behavior. *International Journal of Clinical and Experimental Hypnosis,* Volume 26, Issue 1 January 1978, 22–29.

Bolocofsky, David N.; Spinler, Dwayne; Coulthard-Morris, Linda (1985). Effectiveness of hypnosis as an adjunct to behavioral weight management. *Journal of Clinical Psychology,* 41 (1), 35-41.

Cochrane, Gordon; Friesen, J. (1986). Hypnotherapy in weight loss treatment. *Journal of Consulting and Clinical Psychology,* 54, 489-492.

Kirsch, Irving (1996). Hypnotic enhancement of cognitive-behavioral weight loss treatments—Another meta-reanalysis. *Journal of Consulting and Clinical Psychology,* 64 (3), 517-519.

CHAPTER 10

1.	Sefer ha Zohar: The Book of Splendor.

2.	Many scholars have documented the existence of hundreds of sacred scriptures. How it was decided which were most important and the culmination of what is now known as the Bible has been a subject of great controversy. The following (4) works constitute a small sample of these studies:

Ehrman, Bart D., *Lost Scriptures* (Oxford University Press, 2003).

Ehrman, Bart D., *Lost Christianities: The Battles for Scripture and the Faiths We Never Knew* (New York: Oxford Univ. Press, 2003), chapter 11.

Gamble, Harry, *The New Testament Canon: Its Making and Meaning* (Philadelphia: Fortress Press, 1985).

Mertzger, Bruce M., *The Canon of the New Testament: Its Origin, Development and Significance* (Oxford: Clarendon Press, 1987).

3.   Grant, Michael, *Constantine the Great: The Man and His Times* (New York: Barnes and Noble Books, 1998), 167.

4.   Ehrman, Bart D., *Misquoting Jesus: The Story Behind Who Changed the Bible and Why* (San Francisco: Harper Collins, 2005), 6.

5.   Ibid., 57-59.

6.   Ibid., 101.

7.   Ibid., 209.

CHAPTER 11

1.   Finkelstein, Adrian, MD: *Your Past Lives and the Healing Process* (50 Gates Publishers, 1996), 36.

2.   During his forty years of study, Dr. Stevenson authored or coauthored more than 290 publications. The following (10) include some of his best-known works:

Stevenson, Ian:

Children Who Remember Previous Lives: A Question of Reincarnation (McFarland & Company; Revised edition, 2000).

Where Reincarnation and Biology Intersect (Praeger Paperback, 1997).

Twenty Cases Suggestive of Reincarnation: Second Edition (University Press of Virginia; Rev and Enl edition, 1980).

Reincarnation and Biology: A Contribution to the Etiology of Birthmarks and Birth Defects Volume 1: Birthmarks (Praeger Publishers, 1997).

European Cases of the Reincarnation Type (McFarland & Company, 2003).

Cases of the Reincarnation Type: India (University of Virginia Press, 1975).

Cases of the Reincarnation Type: 10 Cases in Sri Lanka (University of Virginia Press, 1978).

Cases of the Reincarnation Type, Volume III: Twelve Cases in Lebanon and Turkey (University of Virginia Press, 1980).

Cases of the Reincarnation Type: Twelve Cases in Thailand and Burma (University of Virginia Press, 1983).

3.　　Tucker, Jim B., MD: *Life Before Life, Children's Memories of Past Lives* (St. Martin's Griffin Press, 2005), 141-143.

4.　　Hardo, Trutz: *Children Who Have Lived Before* (Rider Books, 1998), 146-173.

About the Author

This is Mr. Scheinberg's second book demonstrating how spirituality may be seamlessly integrated into psychotherapy. The prior work, *Turning Trauma Into Triumph: Ten Stories of Hope and Growth, Including My Own*, focuses on how effective, spiritually-based interventions are utilized in a traditional psychotherapy practice. *Seeking Soul Mates, Spirit Guides, and Past Lives* continues this trend, as the reader witnesses how soul relationships may be the key to understanding what life is all about.

Richard C. Scheinberg received his undergraduate degree in psychology and sociology in 1975 from the State University of New York at New Paltz and his master's degree in social work in 1981 from Adelphi University in Garden City, New York. He is currently a licensed clinical social worker in the state of New York and a Board Certified Diplomate in clinical social work by the American Board of Examiners in Clinical Social Work. Mr. Scheinberg served as an executive board member of the Suffolk County chapter of the Society of Clinical Social Work from 1984 to 1995. Because of his work with graduate students in the 1990s, Mr. Scheinberg was recognized as an Adjunct Assistant Professor at the New York University School of Social Work in January 2000.

Mr. Scheinberg, a psychotherapist with twenty-eight years in private practice helping children, adults, couples, and families, is the director of Sunrise Counseling Center in Bay Shore, Long Island, New York. Founded by Mr. Scheinberg in 1993, the Center now has a staff of fifteen clinical practitioners. Aside from being a human resources specialist for community organizations, employee assistance programs, and managed care insurance companies, Mr. Scheinberg continues to serve as a seminar and workshop leader locally and as a business consultant outside of New York State. He has been featured locally both in print media and on television.

As Mr. Scheinberg has evolved spiritually, he has chosen to devote more time and energy to professional development that is directly associated with what one may call "the life force." This research has included a wide range of training involving mystical and energy practices that relate to life, love, karma, and overall mind-body health. These experiences include ancient and modern forms of meditation, prayer, hypnotism, chakra clearing, psychic development, angel communication, mediumship, remote viewing, and alternative healing modalities (Reiki and Reconnective healing). One of his most important retreat experiences to enhance his clinical repertoire of skills came in the form of training and certification in hypnosis for past life regression from the Dr. Brian Weiss Institute.

Mr. Scheinberg is a member of the National Association of Social Workers, the American Board of Examiners in Clinical Social Work, the International Association for Research Regression & Therapies, and Edgar Cayce's Association for Research and Enlightenment.

Mr. Scheinberg currently resides in Islip, New York with his wife of thirty-two years, Geraldine. They have one son, Jared, who is twenty-seven years old.

Seeking Soul Mates, Spirit Guides, and Past Lives

For more information regarding Mr. Scheinberg and his work, please visit **www.RichardCScheinberg.com** or contact him by e-mail: Richard@RichardCScheinberg.com.

Richard C. Scheinberg, Director
Sunrise Counseling Center
1555 Sunrise Highway
Bay Shore, New York 11706
Tel: (631) 666-1615
Fax: (631) 666-1709

Further copies of this book may be purchased online from LegworkTeam.com, Amazon.com, BarnesandNoble.com, and Borders.com or via the author's Web site, www.RichardCScheinberg.com.

You can also obtain a copy by visiting L.I. Books or ordering it from your favorite bookstore.